Mir

MW01295023

Street

Surviving the Impossible

Joseph.

Joseph Parenti

A True Story

www.miracleon91st.com
blog.miracleon91st.com
Facebook-Miracle on 91st Street

ISBN-10: 149362394X
ISBN-13: 978-1493623945

For my loving mother,
amazing brother Michael,
and wonderful sisters, Diana and Lisa.
Thanks for being there 110% when I needed you and for
never letting me give up or even want to give up.
I love you very much.

CONTENTS

Introduction

The day I survived three heart attacks started off quite normally.

I didn't wake up that morning soaked in a forewarning sweat. No psychic or evangelical street preacher stopped me that day to warn me of an upcoming catastrophe and recommend I head back home to spend the next twenty-four hours under the covers. I didn't have a sentimental instinct to give my mother an appreciative kiss on the cheek, or write a will doling out my meager possessions.

In fact, I felt perfectly fine. I was 23-years-old and had recently graduated college, embarking on a new career as a CPA. I had also moved into my first apartment and started dating a new girl. I was venturing into the "adult stage" of life, although a bit apprehensively. Transitions are frightening; being a grown-up for the first time is scary. But the nervousness I felt at that time was overshadowed by my excitement and optimism.

Accomplishment and pride were among the many sensations experienced as I walked into the office of my new employer each day. The wait to get to this point in my life had been long and tedious, yet it was all starting to pay off. But, as we all learn in life, things can change in an instant. One day, you're going to work with all the promise in the world, the next, your entire life can be turned upside down.

The discovery I would come to unearth that day was this: my birth into this new stage of life would not be marked by a professional job title, but instead by a horrific accident that would completely change my direction and mold me into the man I am today.

Chapter 1

Stop! Thief!

It was a frigidly cold night.

"Help me!" a woman screamed frantically. "This guy is stealing my car!" She ran from the newsstand into the street. A tall, slim man with ragged clothes had forced open her car door and sped away in her blue Oldsmobile. Unfortunately for him, he didn't have a smooth getaway. In an attempt to help the woman, a nearby cab driver, who heard her cries for help, jumped into his car and tailed the thief.

The two vehicles zoomed down Crossbay Boulevard, through Ozone Park and into Howard Beach, leaving many frightened bystanders along the way.

About the same time, I was pulling into a self-service gas station to ready my car for the following morning's commute to work.

Attempting to lose the cab driver, the thief swerved in and out of traffic, ignoring all stop signs and traffic lights.

Undaunted, the brave cabby continued in hot pursuit. Both cars barreled down the streets at high speed, focused only on their dangerous game of cat and mouse—driving recklessly, as if they were the only two cars on the road.

My gas tank filled, I was saying goodbye to a friend I happened to run into at the gas station.

After approximately two miles, the thief made a right turn into Howard Beach on 160th Avenue and his first left onto 91st street. The cabby was still following him close behind.

Both cars, the cab and the stolen vehicle, were travelling well over 80 mph on a street normally travelled at 20-25 mph. They were speeding south on 91st Street as I was driving west on 162nd Avenue.

A few blocks away, I turned on my radio and headed towards home.

As the thief neared that intersection, he did not slow down when approaching the stop sign. On the contrary, he increased his speed, desperate to get away and blinded by the lust of his prize.

Was it fate? Bad luck? A series of unfortunate events? Since that morning, my mind has gone back to that car thief a million times, devising different scenarios. Imagining how things could have gone differently. His "prize" was only a used Oldsmobile. Why didn't he just give up? Pull over to the side of the road, slide out of the door, and disappear into some alleyway? I could only imagine that he was fueled by adrenaline, greed, and the thrill of the chase.

Upon passing the red and white octagon, he pressed his foot down harder on the gas, accelerating the domino effect that would lead to the horrible collision that almost ended my life.

A crime victim, a cab driver trying to be a hero, a petty car thief—I had no link to any of these characters when I woke up that morning. But the chain of events that was set off by each of them was about to change my life forever.

Chapter 2

Fleeing Car Almost A Killer

The following article was published in The Forum of South Queens newspaper on December 10, 1988 covering the accident. It has been reprinted with their permission.

Twenty three year old Joseph Parenti of Howard Beach lays in Jamaica Hospital in critical condition after a stolen car broad-sided his vehicle at 162nd Avenue and 91st Street in Howard Beach. Police officers of the 106th Precinct, Highway 3, Emergency Services Unit; firefighters from Engine Company 331 and 173, Jamaica Hospital Paramedics and the West Hamilton Beach Volunteers were quick to arrive on the scene of this serious car crash, which resulted from a chase of a stolen car, late Monday night.

Apparently, according to the police reports, Diane DiBlasio of Howard Beach got out of her car at Liberty Avenue and Crossbay Boulevard in Ozone Park and left her car running. A 33 year old male/white, later identified as Donald Terkell of 209 South 14 Street, Lindenhurst, jumped into the car and took off south bound on Crossbay. DiBlasio screamed "This guy is stealing my car." Alan Glassman, driver for Crossbay Car Service gave chase through the streets of Ozone Park and Howard Beach.

As the two (possibly more) cars approached the Rockwood Park section of Howard Beach, Terkell turned on to 91st Street, heading southbound. He crossed the intersection of 162nd Avenue "at a very high rate of speed," according to eyewitnesses and broadsided the vehicle driven by Parenti (who was traveling west-bound on the avenue). Metropolitan Protection Services (the private security patrol in Rockwood Park) was patrolling only one block away when they "heard a loud noise from the direction of 91 street and 162 avenue," stated Private Security Officer Salvatore Nesfeder.

"We also observed a male, white, approximately 30 years old, staggering east on 162nd avenue, toward Crossbay Boulevard, apparently leaving the accident scene. Several other males/whites, various ages, appeared to be chasing the first male. The group of males were shouting for security to stop him before he gets away. Security Officer Felix Diaz and I approached the first male to offer assistance, at which time we noticed that he was bleeding from the head or upper face. The male appeared disoriented and attempted to shove me to the ground," continued Nesfeder. "While Diaz remained with the man, I returned to the car and requested the police and Emergency Medical Services assistance."

Metropolitan Protection Services, placed the suspect into their vehicle, awaiting police arrival. Members of the New York City Fire Department and West Hamilton Beach Volunteer Fire Department and Ambulance Corps were dispatched to the accident scene when a person activated the fire department voice alarm near the intersection reporting a car fire and a person pinned. Two minutes after the first alarm was sounded, Metropolitan Security contacted the volunteers directly, confirming the accident.

When the volunteers arrived on the scene (within minutes), members of Engine Company 331 and Ladder Company 173 were hard at work trying to free the victim trapped in the car (later identified as Parenti). One volunteer, David Goldbloom was on the scene before the West Hamilton Beach ambulance arrived and started mobilization. As the ambulance arrived he told Volunteer Captain William Dahl (a member of New York City Emergency Medical Services), the victim has an open head wound, and, was unconscious.

At this time, according to volunteers, Parenti went into cardiac arrest while still pinned in the automobile. New York City Firefighters and volunteers quickly extricated Parenti and started Cardio Pulmonary Resuscitation (CPR). Parenti quickly responded and was then placed in West Hamilton Beach's ambulance when paramedics from Jamaica Hospital arrived on the scene. Paramedics Mark Lobel and Richard Garcia jumped into the volunteer ambulance and started two intravenous lines into the victim. The volunteers, with paramedics on board then took Parenti to Jamaica Hospital where he is listed in critical condition. Sources at the hospital say Parenti has been unresponsive as of press time.

As the volunteers (which also included Lieutenant Joseph Rivieccio and Firefighter Robert McGrath) and city fire department were working on Parenti, police officers arriving on the scene approached the private security for information. According to Nesfeder, New York City Police Department's Emergency Services Unit was first on the scene. Later on, sector cars from the 106th Precinct arrived, as did Highway 3. Nesfeder stated the officers spoke to several witnesses at the scene, then placed Terkell under arrest. Police Officer Gary Muhlenforth charged Terkell with grand larceny auto, criminal possession of stolen property, leaving the scene of an accident with injuries and vehicular assault (which could be upgraded to manslaughter if Parenti dies).

Chapter 3

Growing Up in Howard Beach

I was born in 1965 and raised in a middle class neighborhood called Howard Beach, located in Queens, New York.

Howard Beach is a residential neighborhood with perfectly manicured lawns and tree lined streets. It's located on the southwestern section of Queens, a borough of New York City and approximately fifteen miles from Manhattan. The commercial section, known as Crossbay Boulevard, is one long boulevard that cuts through the center of Howard Beach and has a variety of stores and restaurants. This would be known as Main Street in most small towns, but here in Queens, we had neighborhoods, not towns, and boulevards, not Main Streets.

Since it developed as a residential area in the 60's and 70's, it attracted young couples starting to have children. This resulted in a small neighborhood with many kids around my age.

In this small, close knit neighborhood, everyone knew each other. You knew all your neighbors, some you liked, some you didn't. But you knew them. When you washed your car, one of your neighbors would always ask, "Are you going to wash mine next?" I always thought it was a great neighborhood to grow up in.

I had plenty of good friends; they all lived within a few blocks from me. When we were young, my house was the place to hang out. We played Ringolevio or Manhunt (an adult version of hide and seek) in and out of every yard on my block until one of my neighbors would threaten to call the police.

As we got older, we started going out to bars and nightclubs, always in a big group. My friends and I weren't the type to start trouble, but if there ever was any trouble, I knew they had my back. These friends...these "salt of the earth" friends were by my side constantly during the most difficult struggles of my life.

Unfortunately, Howard Beach came to national attention in the 1980s because of a racial incident that resulted in a tragedy. Three black men were eating at a local pizzeria after their car broke down. They had an argument with some local white teens and racial slurs were exchanged. A fight ensued and two of the black men were seriously beaten. One of the men was hit by a car and killed while running across the Belt Parkway. The incident sparked public outrage and would forever leave a scar on Howard Beach.

The neighborhood would also come into notoriety when it became known that John Gotti, dubbed by the media as the Teflon Don of the Gambino crime family, resided in Howard Beach. Gotti's various trials and ultimate conviction would give the impression that the neighborhood was mob infested with a "Godfather" mystique.

But, for me, these events were in the distant future.

The house I grew up in was a ranch style with three bedrooms and, oddly, only one bathroom. I was the youngest of five children, with two older brothers and two older sisters. It was definitely challenging growing up in a house with five children, two parents and only one bathroom. This meant four men battling three women for bathroom time and, as you might have guessed, the men usually lost.

My oldest brother Richard and my father were able to build two bedrooms in the basement, which helped somewhat with the sleeping arrangements. But there was still only one bathroom. I learned patience, and how to hold it in, the hard way.

My siblings and I got along fairly well. There were, of course, the typical arguments and rivalries, particularly with my brother, Michael. Although it wasn't exactly a Cain and Abel situation, there was tension between us at times. He was only a year older than me and, because we were so close in age, my mom often treated us like twins, buying us the same coats for Christmas and often dressing us the same. At times, it was difficult to assert our individual personalities. Naturally, it annoyed him, more so because he was older. He became more aggravated with our "sameness" when we became teenagers. I remember one incident in particular that seems in adulthood a bit blown out of proportion, but it's understandable when I look at it through the eyes of a frustrated teenager.

About the time Michael turned 17, it became cool for a guy to get an earring. Looking back at the era now, I'm reminded how stringent "acceptable roles" in the neighborhood were observed. It was only okay for a guy to have his ear pierced if it was the left ear. To have a pierced right ear was questioning your manhood and holding yourself up to ridicule.

Michael and all his friends from the neighborhood rushed out to have the same tiny gold earring carefully pierced in the same spot of their left ears. A few weeks later, my friends decided that they wanted to get their ears pierced. Of course, I wanted to get one too. In those days it was all about fitting in—in essence being the same.

When I, the sixteen year old baby of the family, walked into our house, Michael took one look at my freshly pierced ear, exactly like his, and removed his own earring. He never wore it again, and didn't speak to me for an entire year.

It was easier with the others. My sisters Lisa and Diana were always nurturing towards me, after all, I was the baby of the family. My brother Richard was eleven years older than me and he took on an almost mentor-like role.

After noticing that I had a knack for math in high school, it was he who suggested I become an accountant. I remember him telling me, "There are always plenty of jobs for accountants."

Like most families, mine had our share of dysfunctions and secrets that went on behind the closed doors of our white picket fence existence. One of the things that was unknown to me in my early childhood was that my father was diagnosed as being "mentally ill" before I was born. Actually, he was in a mental hospital the day I was born. Many years later, my mother would reveal to me that my grandfather and my uncle came to the hospital to pick both of us up.

When I was 3 years old, my father's mental illness became much worse. Eventually, he would be diagnosed as Schizophrenic. Sadly, he was in and out of psychiatric hospitals and mental institutions his entire life; he was unable to work and care for himself and his family. My parents divorced when I was 4 ½ years old. Therefore, my mother had the daunting task of raising five children on her own for quite a few years. We had very little money, and although she worked full time, she somehow managed to get dinner on the table every night by 6 p.m. To this day, I have no idea how she did it. She's a fighter, my mom. She never gave up, no matter how tough things got for her. I definitely got my drive and tenacity from her. Qualities that I would call on to give me strength throughout the most difficult challenge of my life.

I always felt a great deal of sensitivity and love towards my mother. As I was growing up, I never wanted to give her any additional worries or struggles. As far as I was concerned she had more than enough to deal with. This created an inner drive in me which grew into an intensely serious and determined personality. Her influence always made me want to present myself at my best—and I think that's a good thing. Although, I did at times take it to an extreme; I almost felt guilty enjoying myself while I watched her struggle. I tried not to add to her stress by staying out of trouble, and doing well at school. I started to develop an unusually strong work ethic by always watching and emulating her; she works harder than anyone I've ever known.

I was concerned about being a financial burden on her, so at the age of 12, I got my first job as a newspaper delivery boy. I delivered them by riding my bicycle with a basket on the front that held the neatly folded papers. Waking up at 5:30 a.m. to wrap and deliver newspapers before school wasn't pleasant. When there was too much snow on the ground, I would have to walk to each customer's house while dragging the papers behind me in a bag. At other times, the Sunday papers were so heavy, the bike would easily topple forward while I was sitting on it. It was a pretty comical sight. Since I only weighed about 85 pounds at that time, this would happen quite often.

After two years of delivering newspapers, and breaking at least three windows, I started working at Jack's Stationary Store. I put the newspapers together and handled the cash register for almost two years. I would wake up at 6 a.m. on Saturday and Sunday mornings to work a full day at the very busy store. Although so much effort into pulling my own weight in my family at such a young age was difficult, it also was a badge of honor for me.

I did many of the usual jobs available to adolescents. At 16, I worked at the deli counter in a supermarket; "Is it fresh?" was a question I became very familiar with. Sometimes, I had to fight the urge to say, "No, it's been sitting in the back under a portable heater for weeks."

The following year, I became a pizza delivery boy at a pizzeria called Gino's. At this job, I found inspiration in the owner, who was also named Joe. He gave so much of himself to the business. He took great pride in his work. He was living the American dream, owning his own business! It encouraged me to work harder and I think he admired me for that. I was always striving for independence and freedom.

I was making more money than I had in my previous jobs and as a result, I began to let myself have some fun. I learned that enjoying myself was just as important as hard work; there had to be that balance. I worked for Joe for one year. I eventually saved up enough money to buy his car, which was a nicer and newer model than mine. That was a milestone in my life. It was the very car, a symbol of my determination and freedom that I would be in when I had my accident. One day, after I'd left the hospital, I stopped in the pizzeria and spoke with Joe. I remember him smiling as he said, "I'll never sell you another car."

When I turned 18, it was time to choose a college. Although some of my neighborhood friends would not be continuing their education, it was never a question in my mind that I would go on with my studies. Moving forward. Moving ahead. Improving myself. These were themes that were never far from my mind. Still, because I'd be the only "college man," in the group, I decided it would be better if I went to school away from the neighborhood. It was tough for me to leave all my friends. I knew I'd make new friends; but, it's hard to find a bond like your childhood friends. I pushed myself knowing I had to put my career first.

I started my first year of college in 1983 at the University of Tampa. It was a good school. I enjoyed the experience of being in a completely different environment and having the chance to make a bunch of new friends from different places, with diverse backgrounds and ideas.

What I didn't count on was the enormous pressure that the expense of college would put on me. Tuition, room and board, books. Every time I turned around there seemed to be something else that needed to be paid for.

While my new friends were alternating their studies with carefree, teenage days at the beach, I was working full days, Saturday and Sunday behind the counter at the campus deli. There was a lot of pressure to just keep my head above water, especially since I was only earning about $3.00 an hour. It was tough.

I began to try and figure out ways that would make my life a little easier. The obvious solution was how much money I would save if I was living at home while taking classes.

As if an answer to my dilemma, my brother Michael called to tell me how much money he was making as a waiter in a restaurant in our neighborhood. By now, with the earring incident far in the past, Michael had seemed to put aside his resentment of being lumped in with his kid brother all the time.

After one year in Tampa, I was totally exhausted. I threw in the towel and decided to return home and pursue my education from my home base, the house I grew up in. My mother had remarried by this time—which was, as far as I was concerned—a good thing. I'm a sucker for starting over. For new beginnings.

Michael helped me get a job at Lenny's Clam Bar, a legendary Italian restaurant in the borough. Everyone in Queens was aware of Lenny's, either for a special occasion meal at the restaurant or for take-out. Lenny's always guaranteed delicious, authentic Italian food and it was always crowded.

By working as a waiter at this bustling restaurant, I was able to support myself. The staff at Lenny's would become like a second family. They gave me a nickname, "JP" which would make me feel like an honorary member. It was an enclosed world. We were a team—and I liked the feeling!

I worked there at least three days a week during my last four years of college. The evening shifts were from 5 p.m. to 2 a.m. on weeknights and 5 p.m. to 4 a.m. on weekends. It was non-stop running back and forth, like a mini marathon.

The Lenny's "crew" consisted of approximately twelve waiters, five busboys, five cashiers and four cooks. A special bond had formed between us after working so closely together in such a fast paced environment. Many nights after work we would all go out for a drink to unwind. Like so many close knit work groups, we were like our own club; we had our own inside jokes and expressions.

One of my favorite expressions was: "Check the ice." If another waiter said to me, "Hey JP, check the ice on table 10," that meant there was a "hot" girl or girls at that table and he was letting me know so I could check her out. We were all young and single, so we were ALWAYS looking. I even remember one busy Saturday night when I said the phrase while passing another waiter. One of the newer busboys, who didn't know the expression, actually brought ice to the table. He approached me tentatively with a baffled expression: "Hey JP, table 10 doesn't need any ice." He wasn't part of our world yet, and to us at the time, it was hilarious!

Since I was working approximately twenty-five hours per week while attending classes, I could only handle four classes per semester; it took another four years for me to complete the program. After five years of hard work and study, I graduated from Queens College in June of 1988, with a Bachelor of Science Degree in Accounting. I was 23 years old at that point and looking forward to starting my new career. Prior to graduating college, I had already passed two parts of the CPA exam and accepted a job offer as a staff accountant with a medium sized CPA firm, BDO

Seidman, in New York City. My dreams of becoming a professional were finally coming to fruition.

I was excited to start my career as a CPA, but I was disappointed to learn that after working five days a week in NYC, I was earning less money than working three days a week at Lenny's. I decided to keep working at Lenny's one night per week so I could supplement my income and have some extra money.

Also, I was almost as obsessed with perfecting my body as I was with achieving my academic goals. I felt that a healthy mind, body and spirit were one and the same.

In July of 1988, after working out at a gym in Brooklyn for almost four years, I won the bench press competition for my weight class. At the time, I was a true lightweight, only weighing in at 147 pounds. It was an endurance competition, testing how many times I could lift my own weight. On my first try, I was able to bench press 150 pounds 23 times. Great! But another kid was also able to do 23. Not so great. On my second round, I did 22 reps. Good, but again, my competitor did the same. Not so good. Finally, on my third try, I did 25 repetitions of 150 pounds, while my runner up only did 22. I took first place and it felt wonderful! Although I had never competed in any type of sporting event in the past, I was always very driven to show the world how strong I was, mentally and physically.

In August of that same year, my sister Diana offered me the basement apartment of her home at a very reasonable rent. At that time, it was a difficult decision for me.

Although I was starting my new job the following month, I still had to study for and take the last two parts of the CPA exam. I wanted to have my own place, but I also didn't want to put too much pressure on myself. After much consideration, I decided to move into the studio apartment. I was happy with the decision and started to enjoy my new freedom. I was incredibly excited about my new job and having my own apartment. I'd never been in better shape physically, and was spending my days mentally chewing on accounting problems.

One night, in November of 1988, I met Lily, a beautiful Puerto Rican girl from Brooklyn, at a dance club on Long Island. During our first two dates, we got along great and I was looking forward to our third date.

I felt ready for anything in this next stage of life, but nothing could've prepared me for what would happen next.

Winning the bench press competition

Chapter 4

Driving Into a Nightmare

On December 5th, 1988, I worked a full day at my job with BDO Seidman in New York City. This was my first full time job and my first job in an office setting. After working in the restaurant business for so many years, I was trying to acclimate to this new 9-5 work schedule. Going to bed at a reasonable hour and waking up early was a foreign concept to me.

After work that day, I took the subway from NYC to the Howard Beach station. It was freezing that night as I jumped into my car, a white 1981 Cutlass Supreme, and drove home. Once there, I glanced at my alarm clock to see 6:30 p.m. glowing brightly as I changed out of my dark navy blue suit into jeans and a thick red sweatshirt. I then drove to my favorite place for dinner, Lenny's Clam Bar, of course. It was still an extension of my home.

I had become friends with all of the workers there and grew close with the owner, Joe D. Even though he loved to laugh and have a good time, he also had a serious side and was always very level headed in any crisis. I witnessed this numerous times when the restaurant was a complete madhouse and he would invariably stay calm. Joe D. was definitely the kind of person you wanted on your side if you ever had any type of problem.

In the summer months, I would meet him at the back of the restaurant, where his speed boat was parked. We'd take it out into the ocean and sometimes cruise to a waterfront restaurant for lunch. Some nights, I would stop by just to speak with him. Our conversations ranged from work to dating or just life in general. Other evenings, I would meet him at the restaurant before we went out to night clubs.

In stark contrast to the freezing temperature outside, the restaurant was warm and welcoming. As I walked in, Joe D. was on his way out.

"Hey JP! What's up?" he quickly asked me.

"I came here for dinner. Where are you going?"

"I'm late for an appointment, but I'll be back here about 10."

"Ok, maybe I'll stop by to see you later," I said, as he ventured out into the cold.

I sat in the corner and ordered the pasta primavera, which was one of the newer items on the menu. As I waited for my dinner, I spoke to all the waiters, busboys, and cashiers. I knew every employee well, especially after spending so much time working together. It was a great feeling knowing how much these people cared about me.

The various conversations from different tables combined to create a loud hum. I blocked it out as I sat there eating my dinner and thinking about my future. Everything I had been working for was a reality. Life was good.

Tom, one of the waiters, tried to coax me to go out with him and the rest of the staff after work that night.

I smiled. Tom was a great guy, but I wasn't interested in going out. Although I hated to turn down a night out with the Lenny's "crew," I didn't want to get home too late.

"Not tonight, Tom. I have to wake up early tomorrow. I'm just going to stay home tonight and relax. Next time, though," I called to him as I left the restaurant.

My next stop was the video store. I scanned the new arrivals and noticed the video of Eddie Murphy's standup routine *Delirious*. I quickly grabbed it since he was a favorite of mine. It had been a long workday and I needed to unwind. Murphy delivered; I laughed non-stop. I enjoyed his routine and felt relaxed and content as I lay in bed. I wanted to stay there, but knew if I got too comfortable, I'd fall asleep. I also remembered the car was low on gas. In my usual efficient way, I decided to return the video that night. A seemingly harmless decision that would change the rest of my life.

On my way out, I stopped upstairs to see my big sis and landlord.

"Hey Diana," I said. She was sitting at the kitchen table sipping a hot cup of tea. We had a perfectly casual and comfortable conversation about my new job. I remember feeling grateful to have siblings who loved me unconditionally. If we hadn't been born in the same family, I surely would have picked every one of them as a friend.

The conversation turned to the weather, "Can you believe how cold it is?" I asked.

She rubbed her hands on her arms. "I've got my warmest sweater on. I think it's the coldest night so far this year." Noticing I was wearing my jacket, she asked, "Where are you going?"

"I need to return this video. Do you want to take a ride with me?"

She looked surprised. "It's freezing out tonight!" I'm sure it's not retrospect that makes me remember her looking directly into my eyes, "Are you sure you want to go out there?"

I had this feeling that she wanted me to stay with her, but I had already decided to return the video.

"Yeah, I'll be fine! It's just a little cold, nothing I can't handle," I said smiling. Today, I can't help but wonder why I was in such a rush. It had been a full day. Surely, the videotape could be dropped off the following evening. Why didn't I just join my sister for a cup of tea?

Of course, we all can look back at choices we made—seemingly harmless at the time—that we wish we had made differently.

Once my car warmed up, I started my drive back to the video store. Although the roads were clear of ice, snow or rain, the air was still ice cold. The streets were eerily quiet and completely deserted.

I parked directly in front of the video store. I walked in and saw the owner, Peter, sitting on the floor. I plopped down next to him and after a brief conversation about recent movies, we said goodnight and I hurried to my car.

Back in the car, warming it up again, I glanced at the gas gauge which showed only a quarter tank. *Well, I guess it could wait till morning,* I thought. But then, the responsible part of me spoke up. *Why take a detour to the gas station at rush hour? Be responsible. Do it now!* And it was that part of me that, as usual, won out.

I pulled into the gas station and once again stepped out into the arctic air. As I pumped gas into the car I silently cursed self-service stations.

"Hey, JP, how's it going?" a familiar voice shouted. I turned around and saw my friend Frank. He'd been a cook at Lenny's just a few months before. It seemed everywhere I went in the neighborhood there was a friendly face. As my tank filled, we talked about how we had both moved on to new jobs.

Once my gas tank was full, we shook hands and wished each other good luck. As I got into my car, it started quickly and disco music, always my favorite, blared on the radio.

As I drove away from the gas station, I made a left turn onto 162nd Avenue and travelled steadily west. Since I was on the avenue, I had the right of way; there weren't any stop signs for me like there were for the intersecting streets. I started my ride home with the heat blasting to fight the cold. It had been a great night: good food, friends and entertainment. I was ready for a new day.

In that very instant, a man in a stolen car was about to blow through his stop sign at approximately eighty miles per hour. Everything I thought about my life, who I was, and where I was heading was about to change.

The next few moments happened in some alternate universe. Fast motion. Slow Motion. Reverse Motion. Fast Forward. It all seemed to be happening simultaneously.

I remember hearing honking in the distance. I turned my head and saw a blue car barreling in my direction. I didn't even have time to scream or react. The car smashed into my passenger's side door so hard that the door crushed into my armrest. The back end of my vehicle spun out ninety degrees to the left and ended up on the sidewalk. My driver's side hit the front of a parked car.

Everything went pitch black.

Chapter 5

Killed in a Car Crash

In the close knit neighborhood of Howard Beach, news spread fast—especially bad news.

I was in my dorm room at college when my girlfriend called me and said, 'JP died.' **Jason K, Freehold, NJ**

I lay struggling to survive. For the moment, caught somewhere between life and death. In the coming months the story of the rest of that night would be told to me in bits and pieces.

Ironically, one of the bystanders at the scene was a regular at Lenny's and a friend of Joe D. He recognized me as one of the waiters and immediately ran back to his house to call the restaurant.

Joe D. happened to be next to the phone when it rang. "Hello, Lenny's," he answered.

Sam started right in. "Hey Joe, this is Sam. I wanted to let you know there was this horrible accident down the block from me. One of the drivers was killed, and I think he works for you. I'm pretty sure it was that guy Joe. I think you should come here to identify the body."

"Do you mean the cook?" Joe D. asked.

"No, I think he's a waiter," Sam responded.

Joe D. wracked his brain trying to figure out who Sam was talking about. He couldn't think of any waiter named "Joe." From day one, I was known at Lenny's only as JP. Nevertheless, Joe D. hurried out of the restaurant into his car, racing to the scene of the accident to find out which of his employees had been killed.

Joe D. could never forget that night. Sometime later, he would recall how the moment he stepped out of his car, he was immediately bombarded with noise and confusion. There was a crowd of bystanders, numerous police, fire trucks and ambulances. To him, it looked like some kind of war zone. The bystanders were milling about in the cold, all in various states of distress. Some were talking, others were praying, some were crying.

This was the most devastating scene I have ever witnessed...All we could do was hope and pray for you, our great friend. **Tom C, St Louis, MO**

Joe D. shakily made his way through the crowd. The horrific accident was still blocked from his vision. He worked his way through the gathered neighbors, craning his head this way and that way, trying to get a look at the person who was killed. "Joe? Joe who?" his mind kept racing for an answer.

Then he saw it. My car—familiar to him—up on the sidewalk, a mangled, twisted mess. He realized at once that the person Sam was talking about was me, his dear friend.

He later told me, it hit him like a punch to the gut. He felt the blood drain from his face. He clutched his chest and tried to catch his breath. He ran to the ambulance thinking that it very well might be the last time he would see me.

By this time, one very experienced and knowledgeable paramedic began performing CPR on me, executing chest compressions and blowing air into my mouth. Fortunately, after only three cycles of CPR, I quickly responded to his expert, life-saving maneuvers. Although my heart did start beating on its own, the paramedics were concerned that I had not been breathing for a full two minutes. They understood that the brain can last only a few minutes without oxygen before permanent brain damage occurs.

They knew there was no time to waste. They had to get me to the hospital, and fast. The EMT's then carefully placed me into the ambulance.

Joe D. spoke to a police officer he recognized and found out about the stolen car and learned more details about what had happened.

He realized time was of the utmost importance. He jumped into his car and sped back to the restaurant. He went straight to the telephone and called a mutual friend named Carla. She was good friends with Diane, my brother Michael's girlfriend.

"Carla, hey it's Joe D. from Lenny's. Listen, JP was involved in a really bad car accident, really bad. He was hit by a guy in a stolen car. We almost lost him. His heart stopped, but they were able to bring him back. They're taking him to Jamaica Hospital now. Can you get in touch with his brother Mike or Diane?"

The urgency in his voice propelled Carla into action. "I'll call Diane right now."

Next, Joe D. drove to my mother's and then to my sister's house to deliver the news in person.

Meanwhile, Carla phoned Diane. Carla didn't want to scare Diane and attempted to keep her voice level and remain calm. She informed Diane that Joe D. had called and told her that I had just been involved in a car accident. "Some guy in a stolen car hit him and they brought him to Jamaica Hospital," she added as casually as possible.

Carla's ploy to remain calm was so successful, Diane didn't understand the severity of the accident.

"Okay, Mike's out bowling. We'll go see him tomorrow," Diane replied.

Carla, realizing Diane didn't comprehend the gravity of the situation, lost her cool and dropped her soothing demeanor. "No, Diane!" she asserted. "It's *bad*! His heart stopped, you guys need to get there *now!*"

Diane suddenly grew alarmed. "Okay. We will." She immediately hung up and called the bowling alley, where my brother was with his friends, and had him paged.

Michael was startled; he had never been paged on bowling night before. When he heard his name on the loudspeaker, he rushed to the front desk and grabbed the phone from the hand of the clerk. The bowling alley was noisy, and Michael raised his voice to be heard. "Hello?" he said, unsure what to expect.

"Mike, it's Diane. I'm sorry to tell you this, but your brother Joe was in a really bad car accident. They're rushing him to Jamaica Hospital now."

A thick fog descended in front of his mind. Diane proceeded to explain how the accident had occurred, but to him all of this information was meaningless. The fog only thickened.

The clatter of sounds from a busy night at the bowling alley—laughter, falling pins, idle chatter—formed a deafening cacophony. His mind filled with images of me on a stretcher, blood, broken glass and all the terrible things associated with a car accident. Through the clutter in his mind, Michael tried to focus on the reality of the moment. But the shock of this news, totally unexpected on an average Monday night, caused an uncontrollable rage to begin to build.

Michael's undirected fury was about to burst loose. It took every ounce of his self-control to not start screaming at his distraught girlfriend. He held in his mounting anger and was able to boil down his seething emotions to one simple question: "Is he alive?"

Overwhelmed emotionally, Diane repeated what little she knew about the accident without answering the question. While Michael struggled to contain the anger within, his ears continued to be assaulted with the battering of bowling balls and pins. The noise was becoming unbearable. Frustration grew and joined his anger and fear in their war for dominance over his heart.

Desperately trying to remain calm, he repeated the question he could barely stand to ask, "Is he alive?"

Diane paused and collected herself: "I don't know," she whispered.

Chapter 6

Is he Alive?

Was he already dead and they just weren't telling me? Was he in pain? Was he going to be crippled?
Michael H, Rockland County, NY

Once I was inside the ambulance, two intravenous lines were inserted into my arms. Since this was a life or death medical emergency, the ambulance was required to take me to the nearest trauma center. As they raced through the streets with sirens blasting and lights flashing, my heart stopped for the second time. The paramedics looking after me scrambled to give me CPR, and they were able to resuscitate me once again. My body was on the edge of a complete shutdown, and the possibility of swift and sudden death was imminent.

Just as we arrived at the hospital, my heart stopped-for the third time. But the expression "the third time's the charm" came true for me. The paramedics used CPR once again to revive me and this time my heart continued to beat on its own.

I consider myself fortunate to have been taken to a New York City hospital emergency room immediately after the accident. The doctors in that ER were experts at working with all types traumatic injuries on a daily basis. I was barely alive, unresponsive, and having trouble breathing on my own. I was taking only one breath in the time I would normally be taking at least three.

The doctors in intensive care immediately went to work to save my life. I was hooked up to a system of tubes and machinery that, for the time being, kept me alive.

You got hit really bad and were pronounced dead, but they brought you back to life. **Carla M, Franklin Square, NY**

My brother, Michael, was the first to arrive at the hospital. He always had a strong personality and through the years he had become extremely assertive and outspoken. He charged right up to the desk.

"Excuse me, I'm Joe Parenti's brother. "Is he alright? Can I see him? Where is he?" he said in a rush of words unloading his questions on the attendant.

"I'm sorry sir, but no one is allowed in there right now. Your brother's in critical condition." The attendant replied.

Michael tried to look past her for any clues to where I was and what was being done to his brother.

The attendant slid some forms on a clipboard across the desk. "In the meantime," she said as a way of distracting him, "can I have you fill out this information?"

Michael was exasperated. He knew there was nothing he could do for the time being. He took the forms. He stared at the questions but they seemed meaningless. Feeling helpless, he buried his face in his hands.

Next to arrive was my sister, Diana. There were tears in her eyes. She rushed up to Michael, "How is he? Is he okay? What happened?"

"I don't know. They won't let me see him. He's in critical condition though. The son of a bitch that hit him was speeding. The police said it was a stolen car."

Diana sat down in her chair, shocked, repeating Michael's words, "stolen car, stolen car." She just couldn't wrap her head around the events that led to this moment.

Crying hysterically, my sister Lisa, ran into the waiting room next. Lisa is a very passionate and sensitive person. Richard, the quiet one in the family, came right behind Lisa. He sat serenely in a chair. His face showed none of the turmoil that was going on inside of him.

My mom, Marie and step-dad, Dom came in next. My trembling mother was beside herself with worry and fear. Dom tried to be strong for her, but his eyes were filled with uncertainty and concern.

After only a few minutes of waiting, they suddenly heard a commotion in the hallway. As they all looked in that direction, they saw me passing by on a cot with two doctors rushing me from the emergency room into intensive care.

According to my brother Michael, *everyone got really quiet when they saw you, but I noticed you were moving around on the cot and moaning. I also noticed how muscular you looked. Your arms were huge. After hearing that your heart had stopped beating three different times, seeing you alive and moving around gave me some hope. I started yelling out to you, 'Joe, you're gonna be OK, you're gonna beat this!'*

In time, more family and friends arrived. The waiting room filled with the anxiety of 'not knowing.' The clock ticked, but no doctor or nurse appeared with any kind of update. Everyone was wondering if I was going to make it—although no one said it out loud. There were tears, distracted conversations, and long moments of silence.

The wait for them was unbearable. The worst part was they knew there was absolutely nothing they could do for me. Even though there was no information of my condition, they were horrified at the thought of what I might be experiencing.

After two very long hours, a nurse finally approached my family. "I can take you to Joseph's room now, but I have to warn you, he's been through a traumatic experience and it shows. Are you ready?"

Chapter 7

Traumatic Brain Injury

When I heard what happened...I jumped on a plane, slept at the hospital and a friend's house. I don't even remember if you were conscious when I left a few days later. **Steven B, Glenwood Springs, CO**

They definitely were not ready to see me like this. How could they be? There I was, lying before them, completely motionless and in a coma. The bandages that covered my now shaved head had one small opening with a narrow tube coming out of it. The respirator had another long tube attached to my neck, where the doctors had performed a tracheotomy. The IV was in my arm to give me fluids and medicine. Finally, there was a tube that ran through my nose into my stomach and connected to a third machine that held liquid nutrients.

In addition to me having all these tubes coming out of me and three machines keeping me alive, my head and neck were twisted in opposite directions. The force of the impact resulted in an extreme case of whiplash. My head was severely tilted to the left and my chin was pointed to the right, creating an awfully disturbing appearance.

After spending a few minutes with me, the attending physician approached my family outside the intensive care unit. Based on the grim look on his face, they knew the prognosis was not good. "His body and head has suffered massive trauma. I'm sorry to say this but, he'll be lucky to survive the next 48 hours."

I told the priest, if he was meant to die, he would have died...He's gonna pull through this. **June M, Howard Beach, NY**

As distressed as my family was at the news of the accident—and the sight of my mangled body—the one thing that had been holding them together was hope. The hope that with the proper medical attention, I could and would recover from this catastrophe. The doctor's prognosis hit them like a sledgehammer, demolishing any hope. The reality of my death touched each of them deeply.

What would life be like without someone who was such a vital part of the family in a very special way? One thing they were all sure of, it would be a very different world.

For the next two days, my parents and siblings kept vigil outside my room. They were in a daze and could barely eat or sleep. The doctor's declaration of my impending demise weighed heavy on their hearts. Yet with each passing hour they became slightly more hopeful that my chances of survival were a little bit better. After the dreaded 48 hours passed, and I was still clinging to life, they felt somewhat relieved. Maybe the doctor had made a mistake. After all, doctors aren't infallible. Bit by bit, hope began to return to them. But they still had no idea what the future held for me.

Dr. Nagi, the neurologist, met with them to give his prognosis. "Joseph has suffered a traumatic brain injury and is in what I consider to be a light coma," he explained. "His chances of coming out of the coma are pretty good, but I doubt he will ever make a full recovery. He will have many severe limitations. But, with any head injury, it's difficult to know how much or how little any patient will recover"

My mom had told me 'Your good friend, Joey Parenti was in a terrible collision late last night on 91st Street. He had been revived several times and he is in a coma at Jamaica Hospital.' **Anthony M, New Hyde Park, NY**

The doctor showed my family a CT scan of my brain which illustrated how it was severely swollen. It had actually spun within my skull and remained twisted to one side, similar to how my head and neck looked. "I am very concerned that the swelling is causing severe pressure buildup within his skull."

As the doctor was pointing to the CT scan, the impact of the image of my swollen, twisted brain, and his explanation of the injuries, caused my mother to become sick and dizzy. She almost fainted into my step-dad's arms. He placed her on the empty bed next to mine, and she lay there for several minutes as her senses slowly came back to her.

She listened as the doctor continued.

I had a contusion to the frontal lobe of my brain. This is the area which is responsible for controlling motor coordination, problem solving, memory, language, judgment, impulse control, personality, and emotions.

Dr. Nagi asked my family what kind of work I did, and my sister Diana told him, "He put himself through college waiting tables, and just started a job as an accountant."

The doctor somberly replied, "I doubt he will ever function as an accountant. His higher learning abilities are going to be severely limited. It's a good thing he had the experience as a waiter, because he *may* be able to do that again."

At this point, my family was allowed to visit with me, two at a time, in fifteen minute intervals. It was a relief to them to be able to spend any time at all with me since my condition was still touch and go and they were aware each visit could very well be the last. With their limited time they would talk about the people I knew, the things I liked to do, always adding how much they loved me.

I was in intensive care for three weeks and was later told how excellent the nurses were. They were very attentive to my needs and to my family.

Not everyone on the staff, however, was helpful and encouraging. One doctor scornfully told my sister Diana, "You are wasting your time by speaking to him. He can't hear you."

However, a nurse who overheard his comment urged her to continue. "Your brother knows when his family is in the room." This nurse shared with her that when my family was there talking to me, my brain activity and heart rate would increase. When they left or when the doctors came into the room, all my numbers would drop again.

I do not have any memory of anything that was said to me as I lay in a coma. Nor do I have any definite proof that their loving conversations helped. But I believe that, if my brain activity increased while my family talked to me, their words were reaching me, even if it was in some subconscious transference of loving energy that ultimately built up my will to survive.

My friends took over the entire intensive care waiting room. At any given time, there were about twenty-five of them sitting or lying on the floor, hoping for improvement in my condition. Most of the time, the mood was somber and quiet. I was told it sometimes had the feeling of a peaceful demonstration. My friends did not want to bother my family, so my friend Tony would ask my brother about my condition every so often. He would then go back and relay the updates to the assembled crowd. My room was nowhere near the waiting room so they didn't even get a glimpse of me during their entire vigil.

After the first week, they were allowed to enter two at a time to see me.

I couldn't even look at you, I didn't even recognize you. I remember meeting up with friends talking about you and how you were my first friend in school. **Michael S, Bethpage, NY.**

One night, when the hospital was more crowded than usual, my brother's girlfriend Diane turned to him and asked, "Do you think Joe knows he has this many friends?"

He looked around the room at the number of people who were there for me and answered, "No, I don't think he does."

It's hard to realize how many lives we touch on a day to day basis. I'm extremely grateful that they were all there to see me, stay with me and even talk to me, although I was in a coma. Some sent flowers and balloons, and others brought photos of me with family and friends. They were there for me holding on to the hope that I would come out of the coma and they would see me smile and laugh again.

There were times I cried and other times that I left and we talked about stories about you, kind of like a funeral. **Greg S, Amityville, NY.**

About three weeks after my accident, while I was still in a light coma, my brother Michael was in the room with Diane. "Good night Joe, we'll see you tomorrow," they said as they did each and every night. Suddenly, with my eyes half open, my arm shot up, almost like a wave goodbye. They were thrilled! This was the first time that I had responded at all since the accident.

It was as if they were experiencing a miracle first hand. The entire dynamic of the vigil changed. This started a new chapter. A door was opened. The possibility of recovery was now a reality.

The next morning, I was out of the coma and surprisingly, very alert. However, since I had the tracheotomy, I was unable to speak. My friend Eileen brought me a mini toy computer with a small screen which allowed me to type out whatever I was thinking.

My family and friends were elated. Finally, after three long weeks of not knowing how this nightmare would end, they were filled with relief to see me fully awake. I was aware of where I was and understood some of the details regarding what had happened. Many of their fears had finally diminished. To them, it seemed like the nightmare was over.

Unbeknownst to all of us, it was only beginning.

Chapter 8

Hospital Horrors

The hospital was a trauma center, and needed to make room for newly admitted patients in the ICU. Now that I was out of the coma, they no longer considered my life to be in danger. As a result, they transferred me out of the intensive care unit to the general nursing floor of the hospital. Big mistake. In my opinion, this section was inadequately staffed to supervise someone in my still precarious condition and—within two weeks—I developed five major problems that once again put my life in jeopardy.

- I was immobile and still unable to speak so it was imperative that I continue to have round the clock care and attention. Since I didn't receive it, I developed tremendous bed sores that later became severely infected. Standard hospital procedure dictates that a patient in my condition be repositioned every two hours to prevent bed sores. That was never done for me.

- I contracted pneumonia and it rapidly developed into empyema, not to be confused with emphysema. This exceptionally rare condition occurs when pus gathers in the small space between the lungs and the inner surface of the chest wall and causes an infection. The doctors started me on antibiotics and inserted a tube into my chest in an attempt to drain it.

- One of the medications I was on, called Dylantin, nearly killed me. This medicine, if used properly, can prevent seizures in patients with head injuries. However, it has a tendency to build up to toxic levels in the bloodstream, so it must be monitored carefully. If the levels become too high, it must be stopped immediately until the levels return to normal. Since my blood was never tested for Dylantin in this section of the hospital, the amount of the drug in my system rose to a dangerously high level that was almost fatal. This left me in a complete stupor and it seemed to my family that I had slipped back into a coma. I was completely unresponsive to them.

- With the tracheotomy in place, and the collection of the fluids in my lungs, I needed to be suctioned often. I would start coughing on my own, but I was very weak and the fluid was down deep in my trachea. A nurse needed to use a machine similar to a small vacuum cleaner to suction this mucous out and clear my trachea. This was never an issue in intensive care. But here, on the general nursing floor, the nurses were either too busy with numerous patients or too lazy to take care of me properly.

- My feeding tube would often get jammed up or need to be refilled. My family would try to get a nurse to fix it or place more liquid food in the machine. The nurses would take their sweet time to get there or not come at all. Consequently, I lost 50 pounds in the two weeks I was on the general nursing floor of Jamaica Hospital. This was one-third of my pre-accident body weight.

One day during my rapid decline, the feeding machine beeped non-stop, alerting anyone within hearing range that it needed to be refilled. It was like a hungry infant crying out to be fed.

Let me stress that I had a thin build prior to the accident. After losing 50 pounds, I was nearly skeletal and Michael became alarmed. When no one responded to the continuous alarm from the feeding machine—vital to replenishing my body with nutrients—he went to look for help. Seeing no one in the hall, he approached the nurses' station.

"Would you please come and refill the feeding machine in my brother's room," he requested. "It's been beeping for a long time and he really can't afford to lose any more weight."

The nurse looked up and gave him an icy stare. "Don't tell me how to do my job," she replied haughtily. "I'll do it when I'm good and ready."

That was enough! Michael was blinded with rage. Here was a woman, whose job was supposed to be caring for people, displaying nothing but condescending apathy. Michael exploded. With one forceful sweeping motion, he used his arm to knock everything off her desk.

"You see this," he screamed, pointing to the bottom of his shoe, "this is what you are! Shit!"

Even though he was acting out of frustration and concern on my behalf, hospital security sent him home that night.

That nurse wasn't the only one with an attitude problem. Several days later, Michael was chatting with some friends just outside my room when he was approached by my current doctor, Dr. Chang.

It seemed to my brother that Dr. Chang was saying a whole lot of nothing about my condition and wasn't addressing the fact that I wasn't getting any better. If anything, I was getting worse each day.

Michael waited patiently for the doctor to finish and then he asked, "Why did you transfer my brother out of intensive care? Can't you see how ill he is? He's just not being cared for properly here."

Obviously, the doctor didn't like his authority being questioned. He looked at Michael with scorn and said, "When you go through four years of medical school, then maybe you can tell me what I can do."

This may be difficult to believe, but Michael is usually very good at keeping his cool. But the incompetence and neglect he was witnessing, while my health continued to deteriorate, really made him lose it. "I'm going to rip off your neck," he screamed at the startled doctor, "and shit down your throat!"

Once again, security was called and Michael was sent home.

The next day, I was transferred back to intensive care, but I didn't stay there very long. I definitely wasn't there long enough to make any progress.

When Michael and my sister Lisa arrived at the hospital one afternoon, two of the nurses' aides had placed me on a cot and were taking me back to the general nursing floor. My brother and sister both knew it was imperative for me to stay in intensive care, so they grabbed the other end of the cot to try and stop the aides. With two of my siblings on one side and the two nurses' aides on the other, they were both pulling on the cot as if it was a "tug of war." My brother, Richard, walked in just in time to witness this spectacle and later told me it looked more like a circus than a hospital.

After two weeks of seeing my health rapidly deteriorate, my family was in a state of panic. They could not believe how in a hospital, mere negligence was making me sicker, weaker and nearly comatose again.

I wasn't the only one suffering from the apathy and neglect in this section of the hospital. One of my roommates had a horrible infection in his right leg and was scheduled to have it amputated. Shockingly, on the day of his surgery, someone made a huge mistake and they cut off the wrong leg.

Another one of my roommates was an arrested criminal; he was actually handcuffed to his bed. He was also delirious and kept trying to get out of the bed, but kept falling to the floor since his hand was shackled to the bed rail. Talk about a scary place!

All of Michael's feelings of being protective towards me were brought to the surface and he knew he had to do something drastic and do it quickly. He was exhausted from the five weeks of trauma he had gone through and was having trouble thinking clearly. However, one morning in a moment of clarity as he was driving to work, he came up with a brilliant plan. As soon as he arrived at his office, he called the hospital.

"Good morning," Michael said into the phone using his most authoritative voice. "My name is John Ferguson. I am an attorney representing the Parenti family. I need to know the exact name of the doctor that authorized Joseph Parenti to be taken out of intensive care before his physical condition warranted it."

There was an uncomfortable silence on the other end of the line. Finally, the woman spoke up and gave my brother the doctor's name, Dr. Chang.

"Thank you." Michael responded curtly. "I will be closely monitoring Joseph's condition and you will be hearing back from me. Have a nice day."

That was it all took. By the time Michael arrived at the hospital, about two hours later, they had already transferred me back to intensive care where I was being taken care of properly.

Dr. Chang approached my brother with a look on his face like a little boy who was in trouble, "Your attorney called asking about me this morning."

"Oh really," my brother replied sternly. But on the inside he was laughing triumphantly.

The very next day, Dr. Steven, the doctor in charge of the entire hospital, was my new doctor.

I refer to this hospital as the "after the fact hospital." It was only after I developed problems like bed sores, muscle atrophy or pneumonia, that the doctors and nurses explained that it was caused by being immobile. If someone had simply given this information to my family and friends beforehand, they certainly would have cared for me accordingly while they were there with me every day. It seemed ridiculous to me that the cause of these medical conditions could have so easily been prevented. However, not one medical professional in that hospital seemed to have the knowledge or foresight to see these problems developing and take the precautions to prevent them.

My family desperately wanted to get me out of that hell hole and have me transferred to a different hospital. This was not an easy task. Michael made telephone calls to over twenty hospitals in the New York area, but he could not find one that was willing to take me; they refused to accept a new patient with an existing case of pneumonia.

He was starting to panic, knowing that if I couldn't be transferred to another hospital, I would certainly die there.

Chapter 9

Where am I?

Thankfully, it only took Dr. Steven a week to observe first hand my continuing decline—my weight was dropping and I was getting weaker every day. Perhaps it was with the assumption that he was under a lawyer's watchful eye, or maybe it was just that he was a competent doctor, but he concluded that it was obvious I wasn't in the right hospital. He recommended to my family that I be transferred somewhere else immediately.

On January 14, 1989, almost six weeks after my accident, I was transferred to Cornell Medical Center in Manhattan. According to Dr. Steven, "Joseph is the only patient ever transferred from Jamaica H ospital to Cornell."

After the roller coaster ride of initially seeing me recover from the brink of death, only to witness the steady downward spiral of my health, my family was obviously thrilled to feel I would be in a safe place. Finally, they felt as if they could breathe a sigh of relief and at last watch my road towards recovery really begin.

Michael, Diane and Diana wanted to follow the ambulance to the hospital. They had a strong feeling that if they didn't arrive at the same time and force their way in with me, it would probably be several hours of haggling with administration and dealing with red tape before they were allowed in to see me.

They were all in a state of panic, and it was complete chaos in the car. To this day, Diana refers to this as the "ambulance fiasco." As Michael was racing after the ambulance and trying not to lose sight of it, Diana and Diane were yelling, "Go this way, go that way, don't lose them." At the same time Michael was yelling, "Be quiet! Let me drive!"

Even with all the craziness, they managed to follow the ambulance from Queens all the way to NYC and proceeded to enter the hospital with me. I was immediately admitted to intensive care upon arrival, and taken care of in a manner that had never been provided during my time at Jamaica Hospital. I had serious bed sores by that time as well as a terrible infection in my lungs and mouth.

One petite intensive care nurse, Mary, was very shocked by my condition. She even commented to Diana, "It's almost impossible for me to believe what bad shape your brother is in after spending so much time in another hospital."

After just one week there, I was stable enough to be transferred out of intensive care to the general nursing section of that hospital, where I continued to be given the proper attention I needed. I was placed on an air mattress and the nurses turned me every two hours to ensure my bed sores would heal properly. While most of the scars healed and faded, one became a permanent reminder of Jamaica Hospital's lack of care. Even to this day, I have a scar about the size of a quarter—like a bungled tattoo—on my lower right hip.

It was at this time, more than six weeks after the accident that I began to have my first memories of anything. It wasn't as if I woke up all of a sudden and was shocked or frightened to find myself in a hospital bed. It's difficult to describe the "in-between" state I was in at the time. It was as if I were trapped somewhere between being asleep and awake. Often I would ask myself "Is this real?" or "Am I dreaming this?" I seemed to exist somewhere between two worlds and it was confusing to try and figure out which one I was in.

My family surrounded my bed. They would keep up a steady stream of chatter but nothing really registered. I would grasp on to a word or a phrase, turn it around in my head, but then it would be gone. It just wouldn't register in my brain.

Often, in my blurred, fuzzy, drugged and dreamlike haze, I would feel as if I was floating away. I would rise above the bed looking down on everyone. Sure, I could see them clearly, but I couldn't understand a word they said.

With each passing day, I slowly began to become more alert. Now, I found myself filled with questions. I still didn't know where I was, why I was there, how long I had been there, or even what was wrong with me.

I kept asking Michael, "What happened? Where am I?" He would begin to explain, "You were in a car accident." Then he would add, "It wasn't your fault, you were hit by a man speeding in a stolen car." I nodded dreamily. But the next day I would once again want to know what had happened. Michael would patiently begin the story again. "You were in a car accident..." Sometimes I would ask him an hour later, "What happened to me?" Michael never lost his cool. He'd repeat and repeat. Waiting for the time it would eventually sink in. My head was in a fog and my memory was failing me due to the trauma of the head injury as well as the medications I was on.

When he explained my injuries to me, he told me that I suffered from a head injury, which would be a temporary condition and not brain damage. He stressed that my injury would not be permanent. I accepted what he said, every time he repeated it and never questioned it. His explanation enabled me to believe that although I was in horrible pain, I would eventually get well.

Based on that, and the fact that I was in such a daze, I never had those horrid dreadful thoughts, such as *what if I can never walk again, what if I can never talk again, what if I always need a trachea and respirator to breathe, what if I can't be a CPA.*

I know now that my family and friends did have all the "what could happen" concerns that I was spared. After having the three heart attacks, they still couldn't even be sure if I would survive. And if I did indeed survive, they weren't sure if I would be in a vegetative state for the rest of my life.

The very first thing I can remember clearly was one night when Michael was with me. He was feeding me pudding in an attempt to help me gain some weight. I started to cough, and he noticed that the color of the loose substance that was coming out of my trachea tube was the same as the pudding. He instantly realized something was very wrong. He knew that if the trachea tube was put in place as a direct airway to my lungs, there should not be pudding or any food there.

He requested to see the doctors and tried to tell them what occurred, but they seemed to think he was exaggerating what had happened. One of them even said to him, "No way, that didn't happen."

My brother replied, "Stay here and watch," as he fed me more pudding while they looked on. After eating a few spoonfuls, I coughed it out of the trachea tube again. Once the doctors witnessed it for themselves, they immediately sent me for a video-fluoroscopy, a moving X-ray of my throat and chest. With this test, they could see how the food was moving when I swallowed. After my very first spoonful of pudding, they promptly stopped the test. I was diagnosed with paralysis of my tongue and my epiglottis. This is the flap in the throat which closes off the airway when food is swallowed. I should *not* have been eating.

Since my epiglottis wasn't working, I was aspirating, or inhaling my food when I ate or drank anything. The food was going directly into my lungs instead of my stomach. This was the cause of the infection and pus in my lungs. I blame this on the incompetence of the staff at Jamaica Hospital for never checking my ability to swallow, which they should have done prior to allowing me to eat. Now, after this test, I was no longer allowed to have *any* food or drink.

Once again, I was lucky that I was in such a daze or such an optimist that I didn't think, *what if I could never eat again.* I only understood that I had to stop eating for a while. This was, however, very upsetting to me for two reasons. First, I was furious that this was never diagnosed earlier. If it had been, I would not have been eating and I wouldn't have gotten that damned lung infection. That lung infection caused high fevers, weakness and constant coughing. Sometimes, I coughed so hard, I felt like the trachea tube was going to pop right out of my throat. Now, that's painful!

Secondly, because of the coughing and the trachea tube, my throat was terribly dry and irritated; I found eating the pudding to be very soothing. I wasn't permitted to even have a glass of water, since it is the hardest substance to control for anyone with swallowing problems. All of this was torturous for me.

The next morning, my mother was with me when a nurse walked into my room and approached my bed. "Open your mouth," she commanded. I assumed she was going to take my temperature, so I opened wide-and she threw a pill down my throat! I freaked out. The previous night, the doctors determined I couldn't swallow and now this idiot expects me to swallow a pill. Didn't anyone tell her? Didn't she read the chart?

Of course, I started coughing uncontrollably and looked at my mom for help. She quickly stood up and yelled at the nurse, "He can't swallow ANYTHING, they tested him last night!"

The nurse replied, "Oh sorry," and walked out of the room with an air of complete detachment. She really couldn't care less.

I, on the other hand, continued coughing for about twenty minutes, all the time wishing my mother would have kicked that nurse.

Another early memory occurred on another night that Michael was with me. We heard an alarm in the hallway and saw all the nurses running back and forth past my doorway.

One female nurse ran into my room and nervously informed my brother, "All visitors have to leave now, there's a criminal with a gun in the hospital."

"What?" Michael asked in disbelief.

"The police were chasing him on the streets," the nurse continued excitedly, "but he ran into this building."

"Oh, okay," he replied, in his professional voice. The nurse glanced at me and then at him, confident he would obey her command, and she left the room. I, always the one who follows directions, looked at him and was prepared to say goodnight. He looked directly at me and said, "I am *not* leaving you alone with an armed criminal in this hospital." His protectiveness made me feel very safe, like having my own private bodyguard.

A few minutes later Kevin, a male nurse with a slight build, walked in the room and said to my brother, "I am sorry, but you really have to leave."

Michael, using his protective older brother mentality, gestured to me and said to Kevin, "Let me ask you, if it was your brother, would you leave?"

Kevin looked at me, looked back at my brother, then shook his head and said, "No." He left the room and shut the door behind him so no one else would bother us. Shortly after that, they found the criminal somewhere in the hospital, and he was arrested.

Even with Michael protecting me so much, my head was in such a fog that one evening I got angry with him. For some reason, even before the accident, I never could sleep well while lying on my back. The first few weeks in this hospital, I was lying flat on my back and barely slept. That night, he helped turn me onto my side and I quickly fell into a deep sleep after only a few minutes. The sleep was so deep, that when I woke up an hour later, I was beyond delirious. I looked around at my room and everything looked different. I motioned with my hands and mouthed the words, *why did you change my room around?*

He laughed and responded, "What are you talking about?"

Something felt weird to me so I kept asking him, *why did you change my room around?*

Everything was exactly the same as it had always been and he kept laughing at my loopy behavior. This only made me more angry and upset. When the private duty nurse arrived, I angrily looked at him, pointed to the door and mouthed, *go home.*

After he left, the nurse reprimanded me. "Your brother takes such good care of you, why are you chasing him away?" She kept repeating it, as though she was disappointed in my behavior.

About an hour later, I was more coherent and felt really bad about what had happened. I made a motion to the nurse with my hands that she should call my brother. She did call him and apologized for me; I was glad that he was unfazed by my delirium.

These were not the only memorable things that happened in January. Although I didn't know it, on the day of my accident, Michael had purchased an engagement ring for his girlfriend, Diane. When he went bowling that night, he brought the ring with him to show his friends. I think he planned on proposing to her the next weekend. That never happened because they spent the rest of December at the hospital by my side.

One night, near the end of January, Michael told me he was going to propose to Diane that evening. He wanted me to be his best man and he showed me the beautiful ring he bought her. He left early to take her out for a nice dinner and asked her to be his wife. The very next night,

Michael and Diane came to see me and share the great news.

I looked at my brother and mouthed the words, "Oh, why didn't you tell me?"

"I did tell you...last night. And I even showed you the ring," he responded. At that moment, I had no memory of the night before. I was still in a daze and desperately struggling with my memory. I was happy for them, but concerned about my ability to remember anything, and worried about my future.

Chapter 10

Dr. Doom

During the first week of February, one of the resident doctors, Dr. John, came in to check on me. He was exceptionally warm and friendly with an excellent bedside manner. When Dr. John entered the room, he was always cheerful and smiling and he exuded a positive energy—which is what I really needed at the time. Even when he was just walking down the hallway on his rounds, he'd be sure to stick his head in my room just to say hello. Naturally, my family and I grew to like him a lot.

One day, he stopped in my room with an update. "They'll be removing the trachea tube soon," he said enthusiastically. "So I want to check on how your breathing is functioning without it." Breathing without the tube would've been a big step towards regaining my normal body functions.

Standing next to my bed, he reached over and covered the tube with his finger. I could see he was surprised at my reaction. I was totally unable to breathe with his finger blocking the tube. Within seconds fear engulfed me. Soon I was blinded with panic. Unable to breathe, I feebly tried to push the doctor away from me. My mind was racing, *why is he covering the tube if it's my only way of getting air?*

I didn't understand that if my vocal cords were working normally—as Dr. John assumed they were at this point—I would have been able to breathe normally through either my nose or mouth. It wouldn't have mattered if the tube was covered.

Up until that time, the doctors assumed my vocal cords were working properly. Dr. John didn't understand why I couldn't breathe when he covered up the trachea tube, so he kept trying

He assumed that it had become a habit for me to breathe with the tube. "Joe," he said gently, "You need to try harder. Don't be nervous. Just breathe in slowly."

But, each time he covered the tube, I couldn't get any air and I tried to push him away. Eventually, in utter fear and frustration, I started to cry. I felt like I was being choked and was helpless to do anything about it.

Because of my weakened state, it was impossible for me to stop him. I was helpless, confused, and extremely frightened. Of course, Dr. John wasn't trying to choke or harm me in any way. Scaring me wasn't his goal either. He would only block the tube for a second or two, in an attempt to get me to breathe on my own. Let me tell you, those seconds felt like an eternity to me. I became more and more terrified with each attempt.

At last, when Michael could no longer stand to watch me frantically struggle for air, he said sternly, "Okay, Doc. I think that's enough!"

The doctor stopped. He sighed. It was obvious he was confused. "I'll send the ear, nose and throat doctor to examine Joe," he said. "We need to figure out what the problem is."

The following day, when Diana was with me, the ENT doctor came in. My family, who had met with him before, gave him the nickname of Dr. Doom, because, in stark contrast to Dr. John, he was regularly morose and gloomy. He always seemed to be the bearer of bad news. This time, he was there to examine me and determine what the trouble with my breathing was. The moment he walked into my room, I made it very clear to him and Diana that I did not want him to examine me until Michael was there. After the experience the previous night, I was fearful that the doctors were either trying to kill me, or might kill me...without even trying.

That may sound paranoid, but that was truly how I felt. Dr. Doom went to consult with another doctor, or possibly torture another patient, while we waited for my brother. But upon his return, Michael still hadn't arrived and Dr. Doom informed us he couldn't wait any longer. He approached my bed and, without warning, stuck a long tube through my nose and down into my throat. To say it hurt would be an understatement. Involuntary tears sprung to my eyes. Dr. Doom was just doing his job, but it felt like he was forcing unnecessary, torturous "methods" on me.

By looking through this tube, Dr. Doom was able to determine my vocal cords were not working properly. There was paralysis to both the right and left vocal cords; they would not open to enable me to breathe or speak. He then lived up to his nickname when he told my sister about what he discovered and pessimistically added, "It's been more than six weeks since the accident. If they have not started working by now, they probably never will."

These were not the kind of encouraging words my family felt were necessary to keep the fight in me. My sister, in an attempt to prevent me from hearing his negativity, pressed her finger to her lip, signaling to him not to go on in front of me. Dr. Doom chose to ignore her plea and continued with his bleak diagnosis.

Fortunately, I didn't fully comprehend what he was saying.

I didn't understand what vocal cords were or their function. I was too upset and still in pain from him sticking that damn tube down my throat.

After he left, my sister looked at me and said, "Ignore him." That's exactly what I did. I have to admit that at this point I felt such incredible anger towards him for not waiting for Michael and then sticking that awful tube down my throat without any warning of how it would feel.

I started to think to myself, *what the hell am I doing here?* It was hard to believe that after two months of being in the hospital, they were still finding things wrong with me.

I am sure my poor sister was thinking, *oh no, what if Joe always needs the tracheotomy and can never speak again.* Lucky for me, that thought never crossed my mind.

Dr. Doom came back the next day and told my mother, "If his vocal cords are ever going to start working again, I need to move the trachea tube down into a lower position in his throat. I feel that in the current position it could eventually irritate and prevent his vocal cords from ever moving again."

A few days later, Dr. Doom performed a second tracheotomy, and inserted a new tube in my throat about one inch below the first one. He was then able to close up the original opening.

After the operation, my family still didn't know if I would ever speak again or if I would need to live with the tracheotomy the rest of my life. Only time would tell.

Chapter 11

The Longest Days of My Life

I was truly blessed to have someone from my family with me every day. My mother took a leave of absence from her full time job to stay with me. My sister, Diana also wanted to stay with me, but needed to care for her young daughter. They decided to alternate days between coming to see me and caring for my niece. One of them was there every day for me from 8 a.m. to 4 p.m.

Michael left work every day at 3 p.m. to make it to the hospital by 4 p.m. He stayed with me every night until 8 p.m. My parents also hired a private duty nurse to stay with me from 8 p.m. to 8 a.m. After the disaster at the first hospital, my family wanted to ensure I had twenty-four hour coverage.

My mind was beginning to become more active but my body still wasn't cooperating. Because of the tracheotomy, I was unable to speak. Adding to the frustration, I didn't have enough strength in my arms to write anything down using a pad and pen. This made any kind of communication virtually impossible. It was apparent to everyone that I had thoughts and feelings that I needed to convey. Ultimately, Diana created a letter board for me. I did have enough energy to at least point to each letter, one by one, as I spelled out each word. It worked well at first, but putting together a sentence by weakly pointing to one letter at a time was tedious and time consuming.

After the novelty of me spelling out a few feelings wore off, my family and friends started impatiently attempting to finish the sentence for me. It became a kind of guessing game for hyperactive New Yorkers. For instance, I would start spelling the words *I am hot* and as I got to the "h," they would assume a different ending and yell out, "hungry?" Then they would start explaining to me why I couldn't eat. There they were, telling me why I couldn't have something that I wasn't even asking for. Once again, my frustration would well up and I'd have to somehow try to direct their attention back to the board so we could start over again.

One day, when my mother was with me, the doctors decided to send me for a CT scan of my head. I was placed on a cot and we were escorted to the radiation center. Once there, I was laid out on the narrow table and slid into the small opening for the test. It was dark and claustrophobic and, as my anxiety intensified, I started having a coughing fit. The technician immediately stopped the test to pull me out of the tube.

After my coughing subsided, he tried to slide me back into the machine again, but I wasn't ready! My mouth was now filled with phlegm and I was terrified that while I was in that small, dark space I would start to choke. They couldn't slide me back in there like this! They had to stop it! I did the only thing I could do, which was wave my arms wildly. The technician had no way of knowing what the problem was. Maybe he thought I was just afraid of another coughing fit. He stepped into the hall and brought my mother back into the room. When she was near me, I made some kind of feeble motion with my hand over my mouth. I don't know how—maybe with that intuitive feeling only mothers have—but she understood what was troubling me. She asked the technician for some tissues. She handed them to me and I was able to clean out my mouth.

I thank God my mother was with me that day; I couldn't imagine surviving any part of that ordeal if I was alone.

Everything in my head was murky, mixed up, and jumbled. I still had no memory of the actual accident. My head started devising confused scenarios. I thought that, maybe, one of my friends had been a passenger in the car and was killed on impact. I imagined that my family didn't want to tell me yet. Perhaps, they were waiting until I was stronger to give me the devastating news. The more I thought about this possibility, the more real it became to me. The fear that this might be true kept me from asking them. I wouldn't be able to stand hearing them speak the words. I attempted to figure it out for myself.

I tried to keep track of which one of my friends came to see me to determine if anyone was missing. This was a near impossible task for a few reasons. I still didn't have the strength to write anything down. And even if I was able to keep a log of my visitors, my family would wonder what I was doing. Also, because of my head injury, my short term memory was severely impaired. Most of the time, I couldn't remember who came to see me and who didn't. Several people would pop into my mind that I thought I hadn't seen yet. I would use the letter board to ask about them. My family would remind me that they had visited me the week before—or even the day before. Eventually, I thought about the possibility of someone dying in the car crash less and less. But the worry was always there, just under the surface–along with so many other fears.

All my friends and family had been informed of my head injury. They all knew about my memory loss. Because of this, the first thing they would ask when they visited was, "Do you remember me?" Ugh! I grew to despise that question. It made me feel anxious. I started to think, *what if I DON'T remember who this person is?* Everyone looked familiar. I certainly thought I knew them. But I couldn't remember what segment of my life they were from.

My biggest challenge, was remembering the names of friends from my new job, since I only knew them for a few months. When anyone asked, I just nodded to imply I recognized them. After they were in my room for a while and started talking to me or my family, I would start to get some recollection of who they were and how they fit into my life. Eventually, I knew who everyone was when they walked in the room, but it took some time.

Every single night, friends would come from different parts of my life, Howard Beach, Queens College, BDO

Seidman or Lenny's Clam Bar. It was usually great to see them and I would try having a "conversation" with them by using the letter board. There were a few nights, however, I was in so much pain or so upset, I didn't want to "talk" to anyone. If that happened, I only hoped they understood and would come back another night.

Some nights, there were so many friends there, they would all start talking to each other and stop talking to me. While I enjoyed listening to their conversations and hearing anything other than hospital talk, I was happier when there were fewer visitors so I could enjoy their company one on one.

One night, while my friend Anthony was visiting me along with my brother, one of my hospital roommates had an "accident" and the stench in the room became so bad, Michael and Anthony had to walk out. Because I was breathing through the trachea tube, and not using my nose at all, I was fortunate because I couldn't smell a thing. When Anthony came back into the room, he had tissues stuffed up both sides of his nostrils with the ends of the tissues hanging down to his chin. He looked pretty funny and I started laughing.

When the nurse came in to clean up the mess my roommate made, Anthony looked at her with the tissues hanging out of his nose, and with a straight face casually asked, "How you doin?" I had been cooped up for a long time without too much humor and incidents like this seemed hysterical at the time. Moments of lightness were much appreciated.

Even with my family and friends coming to see me, giving their support, trying to make me laugh, and spreading the love, these were the hardest and longest days of my life. I would cough all day and night because of the infection in my lungs. This made it impossible to sleep. It also caused my throat to get congested. When this happened, I would need it to be suctioned out by the nurse. It would hurt a little and cause me to cough violently, but afterwards I felt a little bit better. I also suffered from very high fevers and my body always felt like it was burning up. I later learned that in addition to the high fever, having all the tubes in my body created additional heat. I would often get alcohol rubdowns to bring down my temperature, which helped somewhat. My brother turned the fan in the room towards me and bought me my own small fan that he attached to the bed. Once in a while, my sister would get me some ice cubes to suck on, although I was not allowed to. I would try anything to just cool off a bit.

Always feeling hot and tired was, as you could imagine, terribly uncomfortable; the days literally dragged on. I couldn't do much of anything, and not being able to speak was quite frustrating. Using the letter board was a big help for getting across a basic message such as, *I'm hot, how are you?* Or *what's my temperature?* But, without speech, any attempt to convey my complicated thoughts, feelings and emotions was futile.

 I had always enjoyed conversation with people. Making my friends laugh was one of the great joys of my life. But that's impossible to do with a letter board. I would get so frustrated when I was misunderstood that I would actually bang the letter board with my fingers to try and get my point across. I was very fortunate that my family simply ignored my angry outbursts. With all the problems I was dealing with, I truly felt that being unable to speak was my biggest loss.

I also had to deal with the odd experience of being bedridden. I couldn't ever recall a time in my life when I wasn't walking. The worst part was how suddenly it happened. One day I was moving around normally, and the next day I woke up in a hospital bed and couldn't get out. It was weird, scary and frustrating at the same time. My right leg had limited movement, but my left leg had none due to the head injury on the right side of my head. One of my daily exercises was to concentrate and try to move or curl the toes on my left foot. It felt harder than lifting weights, and believe me, a whole lot less satisfying.

Also, from laying flat on my back for such a long time, I found myself more comfortable with my knees bent and my feet flat on the bed. At that time, no one knew to place a pillow under my knees while I was on my back. This caused my hamstrings to tighten up and it became difficult and painful for me to straighten them out.

It was impossible for me to know the reason at the time, but the hospital needed to take my blood very often. It seemed like they wanted a new sample every day. The first or second year residents, which I nicknamed "the vampires," were the ones who were sent to collect the blood. Sure, I understood these students needed training and experience, but they were totally inept at taking blood samples. I was so thin and weak, and I had something called rolling veins. As they tried to stick the needle into a vein, it would invariably move away. By their wide eyes I imagined them thinking, *Oops,* when the attempt failed. These young residents would come in and stick me multiple times before finding a good vein. I felt like a damn pin cushion.

One day, one of them poked me so many times, tears involuntarily rolled down my cheeks from the pain. I decided then, I would give each resident only three chances to find a vein. The "three strikes and you're out" rule from baseball. The very next day, a resident came in, tried to find a vein and stabbed me in three different places. Before she could try for the fourth, I put my hand up, pointed to her and then towards the door. I was still unable to speak, and that was my best attempt at a non-verbal, "Get out!"

"I'm going to try over here," she blithely said as she pointed to another place on my arm. I shook my head back and forth resolutely and again pointed to the door. She eventually got the message and left. In a matter of moments, she sent in an experienced doctor who found a vein on his first try.

After that, I realized that the "vampires" level of experience made all the difference in the world. At that moment, I decided not to give anyone else three chances. I was tired of the torment of being a human guinea pig being used to teach residents how to draw blood. From then on, after only one miss, I threw the resident vampire out of my hospital room. Having a little more control of what was happening to me felt really good. My family found it hysterical that I was throwing these resident doctors out of my room. I however, found it empowering.

Chapter 12

Why Me?

Unfortunately, in my physical condition, feelings of accomplishment and empowerment didn't last long. I wanted to feel optimistic but, because I was spending so much time inside my head, feelings of sadness and desperation would often overwhelm me, crushing any hope I had of ever feeling whole again. All of my time was spent lying in bed, helpless and nearly hopeless. Pain, boredom, confusion and uncertainty were my constant companions.

I know I'm not the only person in the world who, when faced with tremendous hardship, started to feel sorry for himself. I was determined not to, but it sneaks up on you. *Why me?* I would start thinking when left alone with my thoughts. I hurt so badly on the inside and out it was inevitable. I'd start to question the reasons for it. I didn't ask my family and friends because I knew they wouldn't have an answer. Besides, painstakingly pointing out the words on the letter board would only underline the reason I was feeling such anguish. Not so long before, I was vital, healthy, and independent. Now, I couldn't even speak for myself.

Why me? Why me? It would run through my head like a chant. I wanted to know why. I wondered, *why was I chosen for this tragedy? Did I somehow deserve this?*

It seemed to me that for my whole life I strived to be kind and always do the right thing. On the night of the accident, I wasn't speeding or driving recklessly. I wasn't drunk! I was only returning a rented movie and filling my car with gas. So I began to question the entire universe, the nature of good and evil and crime and punishment. Why did this happen to me? Why was I singled out for this suffering? Was I being punished for something I had done in the past? I had plenty of time to think about it and I couldn't come up with a single thing I had done that would warrant this kind of retribution.

I also noticed how strange it was that my accident occurred on a Monday night. For the past year, I had gone to the gym every Monday night. The only reason I wasn't there that particular night, was the change in my workout routine, due to my new work schedule. Since I'd just started my full time job as an accountant, I had decided to exercise less during the week and more on the weekends. I was now going to the gym every Saturday, Sunday, Wednesday and Thursday, instead of Monday, Tuesday, Thursday and Friday. Some thoughts of "what if" started dancing around my mind. *What if I'd never started my new job or changed my workout schedule? Maybe then I wouldn't have been in that accident and wouldn't be here in pain.*

As I lay there asking myself these questions and feeling absolutely miserable, it finally dawned on me that I was not helping myself. I could cry and feel sorry for myself all day, but it wouldn't get me my voice back. It wouldn't get me out of bed. It wouldn't help me regain my life. I realized I would never get an answer to the "why me" question, just as the millions of other good people who experience tragedy are given no reason. If I continued to ask myself that, I was just wasting my time and making myself depressed and keeping myself from moving forward.

I realized I needed to immediately change my focus. After all, my desire was to get well and go home, not sit in bed feeling sorry for myself. I thought back to my life pre-accident and remembered how I had always considered myself to be a mentally strong person. Everyone who knew me was aware of my strong will and even stronger drive. I went to school full time, worked a twenty-five hour week to support myself financially and still managed to work out in the gym four times a week. I felt I had a special inner strength. I realized that this accident and my recovery could be the big test I was waiting for to show the world my resilience. It was also an internal battle for me. I wondered, *am I really as strong as I think I am?*

In that moment, I resolved to put all my effort into getting well so I could go home and restart my life. I needed to pull every ounce of my mental and physical fortitude together and spend valuable time thinking and planning how I could get better. I couldn't waste any more time asking myself, "why me?" I now had a feeling that this was a test that I could pass. I knew I would have pitfalls, in addition to the ones I'd already experienced, but I would push forward with the desire to pass the most difficult test of my life. Maybe some of my male ego came into play. It was an extremely tough challenge, but my new attitude was, "I'll show them I can beat this!"

Chapter 13

Good News!

One morning, my mother walked into my hospital room and handed me an envelope. She looked at me with a smile, and said, "You got something in the mail." I glanced at it, and noticed it was from the NYS Education Department. I distinctly remember thinking, *Oh crap! My CPA exam results.* I had taken the last two parts of the exam in November, about one month prior to my accident, and had completely forgotten about it. I slowly opened the envelope and with a lot of effort, pulled out the letter. I could not believe my eyes. I had passed both parts! That was exactly the kind of boost of positive news I needed to keep my focus. I was so excited I hung the letter on the TV in front of me, and showed everyone who came into my room.

Prior to this, I was so distracted by the pain, the setbacks and the general horror of what I was going through, I didn't even think about my career as a CPA. But now, I was even more motivated to get well and continue my new career. This made me incredibly happy.

Sometime later, my brother Richard revealed to me that our mother had actually stared at the envelope for several moments, afraid to open it. She couldn't help but worry. After so many setbacks, what would my reaction be if I had failed? He convinced her to open it. "If Joe failed," he explained, "we don't have to mention it. He hasn't asked about it anyway." After she shakily opened the envelope, she was overjoyed that she could bring me the uplifting news.

Once my current employer, BDO Seidman, heard the great news, they printed up business cards which stated I was a CPA. They did this even though I wasn't yet certified since I didn't have the necessary work experience. Alan, one of the managing partners, came to the hospital to hand me the cards. It was such a remarkable gesture of faith and good will; I couldn't wait to get well to prove to them, and the rest of the world, that I was ready to get started, fully recovered, better than ever.

One night, in early February, my friend Joe D. was visiting. After he had spoken with me for a few minutes, he excused himself and stepped out. When he came back, he told me, "You really need a haircut. Tomorrow night, Claudia and Claudine, are coming to the hospital to see you. Claudine will give you a haircut while Claudia gives you a manicure."

Again and again I counted my blessings; I had such wonderful friends. I knew Claudia because she had worked at Lenny's Clam Bar with me for a few years, but I didn't know Claudine. At the time, Claudia worked for Claudine at her hair salon in Howard Beach.

The next night, the two busy women took time out of their schedule and came to the hospital. And, wow, was it a special treat to see them. They were both beautiful brunettes with big brown eyes. My brother Michael immediately adjusted the bed so I was sitting upright. Prior to this, I was almost constantly flat on my back or, at most, on a very slight incline. It felt terrific to be sitting upright. Claudine started cutting my hair and Claudia began the manicure. It really lifted my spirits, being pampered by these two lovely ladies.

Unfortunately, after sitting up for about ten minutes, I started to feel dizzy. I tried my best to ignore it, but it kept getting worse. Finally, I had to let them know that we had to stop because I was beginning to feel nauseous and faint. Reading my signal, my brother lowered the bed until my head was horizontal with my body.

Undaunted, Claudine continued to cut my hair while I was flat on my back. I don't know how she did it, but she did a great job. Claudia also finished my manicure. What a team. It was these kinds of acts of kindness that really made a difference during an extremely difficult time. I will be forever grateful.

BDO SEIDMAN

15 Columbus Circle New York, NY 10023-7711

Memorandum

Date: February 7, 1989

Re: Joe Can Have Visitors!

Alan visited Joe Parenti and I'm pleased to report that Joe is making excellent progress. The road ahead is still a long one, but Joe is gaining strength each day.

Joe very much appreciates cards that he has received and looks forward to hearing from his friends at BDO Seidman.

Joe can have visitors - limited to one or two at a time.

Visiting hours are from 11 A.M. to 8 P.M.:

Room 701 Whitney Pavilion
New York Hospital- Cornell Medical Center
York Avenue @ 68th Street

A special note: Joe has passed the CPA Exam.

Internal Memo from BDO Seidman

Chapter 14

The Kiss of Life

A few weeks later, near the end of February, I was able to begin physical therapy. Being in bed for over two months had done a number on my body, leaving me extremely weak physically, and very emotionally vulnerable. I had never felt so frail. I was still 50 pounds less than my pre-accident body weight.

The two physical therapists assigned to treat me were Sandy and Maureen. These two women were complete opposites. Sandy was very pretty, with long dark hair and a very gentle approach to therapy. Maureen, on the other hand, had a severe appearance and a militant demeanor to match. She was obnoxiously stern with me. I would go so far as to say Maureen was borderline mean.

Sandy's role was to eventually get me to walk. Obviously, we'd have to begin by getting me to the starting point of being able to stand by myself. I had to think about that for a minute. I let it sink in: *I can't even stand up by myself.*

"Don't worry, Joe," Sandy said to me softly. "We'll do this in baby steps." Baby steps indeed. The first step we took was trying to raise the bed to an upright position so I could sit up without getting dizzy. This was something I was still unable to do.

We began slowly. Sandy was so compassionate and patient with me; I really enjoyed working with her. Her demeanor made me feel calm, relaxed and determined to improve. At first, I could only sit up for a short time before I started to feel light headed. Everything starting spinning around. *Oh no, no,* I thought. *Not so soon.* But overcome with dizziness, I would have to lie back down until the lightheadedness subsided. Then I would sit up once more. We repeated this several times during each session. We would meet every day for one hour, and each time I was able to sit up a bit longer. Finally, after two weeks, I was able to sit up without feeling any dizziness!

When this happened for the first time, an inner confidence blossomed throughout my entire body. It brought me back to the day I won the bench press competition for my weight class. The feeling of triumph was a terrific motivator.

If Sandy was a bright light in my long and twisted road to recovery, Maureen started off as a dark cloud. I suppose if I were to take a page out of the "everything happens for a reason" book, I can rationalize that I needed some toughness to balance out Sandy's sweetness. The very first day Maureen came to see me, I could sense she was going to be difficult. She had an imposing air. She glanced at me, and then at Diana, who was waiting with me, and barked out, "What's wrong with him?"

My sister began to recite the by now familiar story. "He'd been in a coma, got very sick afterwards with pneumonia and has been in a bed for about two months."

Maureen raised her eyebrows in surprise. To me it looked like she had a condescending smirk, as if what she was being told made absolutely no sense and she was dealing with lunatics. "Okay," she said at last, "But why can't he walk?"

Diana and I looked at each other. We were simultaneously thinking, *what kind of therapist is this tyrant? Doesn't she understand the effects of being in a coma?*

This physical therapist kept asking the same question, like a nagging toddler who doesn't understand why she can't have candy for breakfast. Eventually, frustrated with getting the same answer, she left the room to go examine my file, probably in hopes of understanding why I couldn't walk. Diana and I stifled a laugh. The woman was ridiculous.

When Maureen came back into the room, she explained why she was so confused. "I had training in Europe. There, if a patient is in a coma, the therapists pick him up out of bed and walk him around right away, while he's still comatose."

My eyes grew wide as she explained things that had never occurred to me. Maureen, with all her gruff, condescending demeanor, was not so ridiculous after all. Bed sores, pneumonia, and muscle atrophy could all be prevented when this is done. She continued, "When the patient does wake up, his recovery time is much shorter."

Diana and I were absolutely shocked. We had never heard of this kind of treatment.

I wondered how much faster my recovery time might have been had I been given the European method of treatment.

The information gave Maureen a little more credibility in my eyes. I put my faith in her. I started working with her on my twisted neck issue. It was still locked in one position, tilted to the left and impossible for me to move it due to the trauma and whiplash. To compensate, I unknowingly tilted my body to the right. If I didn't, the world would have looked crooked through my eyes. With my neck and body twisted in opposite directions, my eyes and head were level and everything looked fine.

When Maureen attempted to straighten my head out, my body remained tilted to one side and I felt crooked. "Try and hold your head straight," Maureen persistently told me. In spite of wanting to correct my twisted neck, I just couldn't; it wouldn't budge. The whole time I felt rigidly locked in one position. It was terribly frustrating to hear her telling me, "Keep trying" or "Try harder," in a tone that conveyed that she was under the impression I was being lazy. I was anything but lazy! I was already giving it everything I felt I had. I was trying as hard as I could. But no matter how intently I tried to hold my head straight, it simply would not budge. I kept working at it, though, pushing myself, because I saw what the patience and persistence of my work with Sandy had accomplished.

One day, a few weeks after working with her, she looked at me and said, "It really shouldn't be taking this long for you to hold your head upright." I thought to myself, *is she kidding me*. I used the letter board and slowly pointed to the letters, *Rome was not built in a day*. I wasn't trying to be funny or sarcastic, I was just being realistic. I only wished she would be more realistic...and compassionate!

When my sister Lisa came to visit a few times from Georgia, she would always spend the entire day with me. She would arrive at 8 a.m. with my mother or Diana and leave at 8 p.m. with my brother. Lisa, who was trained as a chiropractor, would always spend some time working on my neck. She did not give me any kind of adjustment, but would try to stretch my neck and move it around as well as she could. She was concerned that it could stay permanently locked in one position if it wasn't continually worked on.

Maureen walked in on this one day and snapped, "You know, if the insurance company finds out your brother is being treated in this hospital by an unauthorized medical professional, they could deny any further coverage." She must have felt threatened by my sister, who was only trying to help me.

I remember Lisa getting upset after hearing this and I used the letter board to tell her, *don't worry about her, she is only jealous because you know more than she does*. My poor sister spent 12 hours a day trying to help me and this idiot was making her feel bad.

Despite not getting the best results with my neck, I was doing pretty well with my legs. Once I was able to sit up without getting dizzy, I started getting out of bed and standing with Sandy's help. I would sit up and throw my legs out of bed while holding tightly on to her arm in an attempt to stand up. She then had me put my arms around her neck as I tried to rise. Although I rather enjoyed this, because she was so pretty, I could only stand for a few seconds at a time. We did this over and over to build up the strength in my legs. Slowly, with practice, I was able to increase those seconds to minutes.

As soon as I was able to get out of bed with some assistance, Sandy decided to try and get me into a wheelchair. Of course, there were problems with this. The first one was the tremendous bed sores on my skin, which made sitting in a chair very painful. To solve this, the nurses found me a big orthopedic wheelchair. This one had a nice thick cushioned seat, and the ability to turn into a bed with the touch of a button. Therefore, I could sit in the chair for about five to ten minutes, before my sores started to hurt. Sandy would then press the button and make the chair go flat. This allowed me to lie down for a while, until I was ready to try again. I slowly tried to increase the length of time I was able to sit up.

The second problem was my twisted, extremely weak neck which Maureen was trying to help me with. It was still tilted to one side and I couldn't hold it upright, even when I used the orthopedic wheelchair, which had a very high back.

This problem was solved by my sister, Lisa. She used a sheet to wrap around my forehead like a bandana. Instead of tying the knot behind my head, she secured it to the back of the chair so my head was actually strapped to the chair. I could only take this for short periods because of the pain and discomfort. Additionally, whichever family member was with me would sometimes use their hands to hold my head up when I wanted a break from the "sheet around the head" method.

I felt ridiculous, helpless and humiliated with my head strapped to the wheelchair. I kept thinking of how only a few months earlier I had won the bench press competition and now my head was being held up by a sheet. It was a very upsetting thought, so I tried hard to block it out. It wasn't the only embarrassing part of the healing process. Because of my condition, I needed to use a bedpan, which was not only humiliating but also uncomfortable and painful. Since I only weighed one hundred pounds soaking wet, I was afraid I'd fall in!

Thankfully for me, there were also some nice bright spots to help balance out the difficulties. Even though Lily—the girl I had met shortly before the accident—had only been on a few dates with me, she visited me at Cornell Hospital. My family told me she had also visited me at the first hospital, but I had no memory of anything that happened there. Lily came to see me every few days, and each time I tried to ask her questions using the letter board. Of course, our conversations were limited, but I was extremely grateful to have this lovely, friendly young lady, there to give me support. She also talked warmly to Michael and my friends, even though she hadn't met them before.

One night, Michael and Lily were my only visitors. I got into the wheelchair and my brother wheeled me into the solarium. He left Lily with me while he went to get a cup of coffee.

We once again took a stab at conversation. She'd say a few words and I would slowly try to respond pointing at letters on the mini letter board. It was awkward and tedious. I felt tension filling the room—thinking that maybe she was getting bored with the conversation, the situation, or with me. But then, suddenly, unexpectedly, she leaned over and gave me a sweet, brief kiss. My heart raced. My palms became sweaty. It had been such a long time since my body received any pleasant sensations—it affected me like a delicious drug being injected into my veins. Then she kissed me again, but this time it was longer and more passionate. As we were kissing, a thousand thoughts raced through my mind, like, *I cannot believe how good this feels. I hope it never stops.* At the same time I couldn't help but self-consciously wonder, *how could she possibly want to kiss me?* I knew my appearance wasn't too attractive at the time. We kissed for quite a while, my head pleasantly spinning throughout. Even after we stopped, I continued to feel as if I were floating. I felt exhilarated, like a child seeing snow or the ocean for the first time. It was beautiful. It was surreal. It was life affirming!

My brother eventually came back to take me to my room, and Lily left for the night. Once Michael and I were alone in the room, I used the letter board to let him know about the kissing. He smiled at me and said, "Way to go."

The next night, when he came back, he asked me again about the kissing. "My girlfriend is concerned you were maybe delirious and imagined it. How were you able to kiss with the trachea tube and your twisted neck?"

I used the letter board to let him know that although my neck was twisted, we still managed. I also wrote how the trachea tube was not a problem either. It enabled me to continue breathing while we kissed!

Lily continued to visit me every few days. Through all the pain and agony I was experiencing, this was a welcome distraction. We all have heard about the power of a kiss: in fairytales, in poetry, in the movies. But I experienced that power in real life. As if it held magic power, it motivated me to strive, strive even harder. To find the energy somewhere in me that I hadn't utilized yet. Most of all, it made me envision myself again in a normal life.

Chapter 15

Under the Knife

Although I was making some progress in my physical therapy, I still felt like a very old man—sick and weak—while my mind remained young and hungry for new experiences. I can't impress on you how desperate I was for my body to catch up with feeling the same way my spirit did.

The main complication delaying my recovery was the infection in my lungs, which caused high fevers and chronic coughing. That, coupled with the weight I had lost, made it almost impossible for my body to grow stronger.

Ultimately, the doctors decided to operate and surgically remove the pus and staph infection. The reasoning was perfectly logical: their initial treatment for clearing the infection was to have a steady stream of antibiotics pumped into my system through the IV and the chest tube in place to drain the infection. After two months of this, however, it became clear that this alone would not rid my body of the intractable infection. There was the added concern that leaving the chest tube in my body for such a long time could possibly cause a secondary infection. In my condition, that could be catastrophic.

They planned on cutting into the side of my chest and removing half a rib, so they could get to and eliminate the infected pus in my lungs. When they first told me about the operation, it seemed like a good idea. I knew if they could get rid of that infection, my recovery would be much quicker.

But as I thought about it, my complacency regarding the operation turned into a dull shock. I imagined my frail body being opened up. Hadn't I been through enough? The more I thought about it, the more shocking the idea became. Then the shock mixed in with panic and discouragement. I wasn't sure if my body could even handle another surgery. I couldn't help but think back to the days that I had worked in the deli at the supermarket. I felt like a piece of meat to be laid out on the butchering slab: "Let's cut him here a little, some over there and don't forget to slice him right here again—and we'll take a rib while we're at it."

This was also very upsetting to me because I knew that although my body had recently started to get a little stronger with the physical therapy, another surgery would only drag me back down to square one. I didn't want to put my body through any additional trauma. In addition, all of my previous operations were done when I was either in the coma or not aware of what was going on. There's something to be said for oblivion. This time, I was fully aware of my circumstances and had too much time to think and worry about it. I was an emotional mess.

Michael tried to convince me that the operation was for the best. "This is a small step back for three steps forward." His words calmed my fears.

The way he explained it, I'd be laid up again for a while, but once the infection was removed, the physical therapy and recovery process would move along much faster. Obviously, this made sense to me. Our goals were the same. I wanted to get better and go home. The operation seemed like the fastest route. But, every time I thought about it, I became agitated. Full of doubts. Afraid. Still, I realized I really had no other choice.

But life wasn't done playing games with me.

One morning, a few days before the scheduled procedure, a resident doctor came into my room. "Did you hear the good news?" he said smiling. "No operation for you." He didn't give me any reason for the sudden change of plans before he left, but I was thrilled. *Maybe the antibiotics have kicked in,* I thought. Actually, I really didn't care about the details. Tears started rolling down my cheeks because I was so relieved at the thought of not having another surgery. I couldn't wait for some family member to come in so I could tell them the good news. *No operation!* But as I was waiting, the news changed again.

About an hour later, the doctors were making their morning rounds when one approached my bed. He had no clue I had heard anything regarding the operation. "We decided to postpone your surgery," he said, stone-faced. "We're going to wait until you're a bit stronger."

There was no way I could accept this news. Nope. No way! I had been laying there for an hour, overflowing with relief that the operation was called off. The resident had given me no indication that it was only going to be delayed. I tried and tried to convince the doctor that he was making a mistake. I don't know who I was trying to kid. I guess myself. After I settled down, the doctor made it perfectly clear that the operation would most definitely take place. It was merely postponed for the time being.

So what I had thought was good news had turned out to be much worse. Because now my recovery plan was delayed yet again. On top of that, I had more time to think about the operation, wallowing in fear, and devising scenarios in my head regarding all that could go wrong. I had already beat death a few times. I wasn't a gambling man. I didn't feel up to taking another chance at life's fickle roulette table.

About two weeks later, the dreaded day of the operation came. I tried to remain calm but it's hard to relax when you're flat on your back being wheeled down sterile halls with your head filled with the knowledge that your body is going to be cut open. *I'll close my eyes,* I told myself. *And when I open them again, it will all be over.* I took a deep breath.

General anesthesia was used so I didn't feel a thing and don't remember much about it. I quickly went under. About two hours later, I woke up. I was heavily sedated and my brain was in a fog. But I was alive! I looked around and thought, w*here am I?*

"You're in the recovery room," the attending nurse told me, "You have to stay here for three more hours."

As usual, my family was the first thing that came to my mind. I made a motion with my hands for her to call my room. The doctors had originally said I would be back from recovery in two hours, which had already passed. I knew someone was waiting for me in my room, and I didn't know what time I would be there. I laid there and slept a little, but I couldn't wait to see my family. After a few hours, I was taken back to my room and my brother and mother were there. It was a pleasure to see them, but our visit was cut short. Filled with relief that I made it through and my family was nearby, I fell into a deep, pleasurable slumber.

I was in bed following the operation for about seven days with a high fever and on strong pain killers; I did not have any physical therapy during that time. Once again, I had a tube placed into my chest for drainage. That pain was by now familiar, but no less extreme. After about one week, I started to feel a little better and gradually resumed physical therapy.

Of course, I was delighted to start therapy again. Yet, at the same time I was beyond frustrated. I had come so far prior to the operation. Now, I saw my carefully built house of cards scattered on the floor. One by one I had to rebuild. I had to learn how to sit up again. I couldn't do it without help. *You gotta be kidding me,* I said to myself in disbelief. I also tried to take a few steps but I needed a lot of assistance—much more than I needed before the surgery. This was the true meaning of "baby steps."

There was a part of me that wanted to just give up. My whole world had crashed down upon me in one night.

Every single time I tried to rebuild, it seemed like I was smashed down again. You try to fight it off, but the self-pity sneaks up on you. I again started to think about how unfair it was. I realized I should have been happy that I was even still alive after what I had been through, but in that moment, I couldn't appreciate it. I started to wonder, *maybe I should have just died in that accident.* It would have been easier than living through all this shit!

Miraculously, after that first week, my fever began to finally drop and I again started to gain weight. I hadn't realized how much that infection was holding me back. Once it was gone, I started to feel mentally and physically stronger every day.

At last, I was starting to gain some strength in my left side. Since I am left handed and I had temporary paralysis on that side of my body, it had previously been impossible for me to write. Any two-year old can hold a pen, but I couldn't. After the operation, and with a great deal of practice, I was able to grasp the pen, write some messages, and eventually even a few letters to some friends. Scrawled, scribbled and sloppy, but they were still legible. I was so happy that I now had the option of either using the letter board or writing a message to communicate.

In addition to improving physically, some of my memory was slowly coming back. During this time, I started to realize that after spending so much time in the hospital, I actually felt comfortable there. I was in a familiar routine, and thought, *wow, this is my life now,* but I didn't want this to be my life. I didn't want to get comfortable and reliant on a hospital to sustain me. The more I saw my friends, looked at photos and remembered things from my past, the more I realized I had a non-hospital life before this. I had gone to school, worked, and had plenty of fun. Now, it all seemed so far away, almost like a dream. I wondered, *where did all that go?*

At times, it seemed like only yesterday that I went out to a nightclub, danced, and had drinks with my friends. Yet, here I was, stuck in bed, unable to get up or talk. My life had turned around completely so very quickly. I never dreamed something like this could have happened to me. It all changed so unexpectedly. I didn't see it coming. But no one ever does.

I tried to make the best of my circumstances, but it wasn't easy. Part of what helped my situation was how incredibly privileged and blessed I was to have my friends and family by my side constantly. Frankly, I don't know how I could have endured that long horrible nightmare without them.

While they were with me, I attempted to convey some funny thoughts using the letter board or by writing a note. "If the doctors wanted ribs," I joked, "they should have ordered Chinese food."

I remember I enjoyed watching *I Love Lucy* every morning from 9 a.m. to 10 a.m. Thank God the perennial red-head was in morning syndication during that time and her hare-brained antics took my mind off my struggles for an hour. Some of my friends brought me books to read, but that was difficult because my concentration was a shambles. Michael brought in my Nintendo game, but couldn't hook it up to the hospital TV. That was too bad, because it would have given me something to do while lying in bed most of the day.

Sometimes, during the night, I would try to distract myself by picturing a normal life. I would see myself out dancing, working out at the gym or even waiting tables at Lenny's. I don't know if I was replaying old memories or trying to create new ones. When I watched these images or stories in my head, it strengthened my desire to have a normal life again. I think that by seeing myself as being well, it helped my mind believe and achieve wellness.

With the feeding tube working properly, I was gaining some weight, but it was happening slowly. Everything was happening slowly. My once fast-paced life was now unfolding in slow motion. I knew I somehow had to accept this new life of mine and tried to laugh as much as I could to get through each day. Sometimes it was a forced laugh, more like the memory of what a real laugh was, but it was a reasonable facsimile—and better than no laughter at all.

Since I had asked Michael about the accident numerous times, I knew and understood the story pretty well. After the thief stole the car, a cab driver chased him for about one mile until the thief slammed into me. I didn't give either of these two people much thought while I was in the hospital. I was overwhelmed with anger because of the situation I was in, but for some reason, I didn't think about or direct any anger towards them.

That was until one day when a social worker came into the room and started asking me some questions. The most jarring question she asked was, "Do you ever think about taking your own life?"

Perhaps, if she had asked me weeks before, when I was at my lowest point, my response would have been different. But, at that moment in time, the question seemed utterly ridiculous. I was struggling every moment of every day to stay alive so I could get better and go home. Why would I want to end it now?

I thought, *if anyone should be punished it should be that thief or even the cab driver for chasing him.* I understood the cab driver was trying to help, but I felt like the two of them were responsible for the tragic situation I was in.

It was as if thinking about those two men lit a fire in me. The more I allowed my mind to think about them, the higher the flames rose. I had to be careful, to not let the flames of anger burn me, to consume my positive energy and affect my motivation for getting better, back to the dream that once was my life—and making it a reality again.

Chapter 16

Finding My Voice

A few weeks after the chest operation, Michael was visiting with his girlfriend Diane. After one of my coughing fits, she looked at my brother. "His cough sounds different now," she said excitedly. "I think his vocal cords may be working." Michael, with his usual efficiency (which never ceased to amaze me), immediately requested that the ENT doctor come to check me out for any changes as soon as possible.

The following evening, Dr. Doom came to my room to examine me and he again stuck that wretched long tube through my nose and down into my throat. This time, however, he did see some movement. "Breathe in," he told me. Then while he held his finger over my trachea tube he told me to say, "One, two, three."

I tried it and to everyone's surprise, especially my own, I was able to repeat the numbers out loud. Michael and I automatically looked at each other and grinned with triumph. Then the doctor had me try it with A, B, C. Again, I was able to do it. My voice was very hoarse and the words were slurred, but I had spoken for the very first time in three months! My vocal cords were getting some movement back. I didn't fully understand what that meant, but any progress gave me a tremendous boost of confidence and energy. Rays of hope were starting to shine through the clouds of depression and frustration.

My brother was elated. He understood—in a way I couldn't—what was beginning to happen. Michael had been well aware that there had been a chance I would never speak again. Now, he was able to discard that terrible possibility. "Joe can talk again," he would announce proudly as visitors arrived.

Realizing that my vocal cords were finally starting to work, Dr. Doom came back the next day and replaced the trachea tube with a narrower one. By doing this, I would be able to become more and more comfortable breathing on my own—without the assistance of a tube.

After that, anyone who came to visit me asked me to speak for them. "Say something, Joe," they would invariably ask as they entered the room. Then they would stare and wait, as if I might recite. I understood that they were eager to see my improvements for themselves, but still it made me feel uncomfortable. It was as if I were a newly trained dog. "Speak!" I got to the point where I didn't want to talk for anyone. I may have said, "Hi," here and there to a few people, but that was it.

One evening, after everyone had left and I was alone, the phone started to ring. I picked it up and just listened. It was my sister Lisa, who lived in Georgia at the time.

"Hey, little brother. I hope you're okay. Can you speak to me?"

At first, I was silent while listening to her, but then I decided to try talking again. I felt more comfortable without anyone standing over me and staring as I struggled to form my first words. I think Lisa was almost ready to give up on me when I uttered the word, "Hello." It was not easy. I had to breathe in, use my finger to cover the trachea tube while I spoke, then remove my finger to breathe out. Then do it again. I started putting some words together. And that led to a few wobbly sentences. Although it was difficult, I was excited and happy as the words formed. I surprised us both that night with the sound of my voice.

Considering that I had not uttered a word for almost three months, I did relatively well. Even though I was difficult to understand, Lisa managed to figure out what I was saying and we were both bursting with happiness at this major breakthrough. Regaining what I had considered to be my greatest loss was not only uplifting, but also gave me renewed strength and urged me to push further. As the thought of being able to finally speak again sunk in, I truly felt more empowered. I hadn't realized how valuable such a simple action was in my life until I lost it. After experiencing how difficult it was to express myself without speaking, being able to do it again made it that much sweeter.

As the days passed, I still didn't feel comfortable talking in front of anyone, but I was fine speaking on the phone. Thinking back, it seems strange to me now, but at the time it made perfect sense. I spoke with Lisa the next few nights, and then began calling other people that I knew. I called Lenny's Clam Bar and talked to some friends. The more I talked, the better I sounded; I also started to feel more comfortable with my new voice. Soon after, I felt more relaxed and began speaking in front of my friends and family.

Although I was now able to speak briefly to family and friends, I still wasn't comfortable speaking to the doctors or nurses. Since my voice was still weak, I was unable to sound confident or demand something when I needed to.

I was finding my voice, and I rejoiced in that. Now, I needed to find a way to regain my confidence.

Chapter 17

Nurse Ratched

As I mentioned, my parents hired private duty nurses to stay with me from 8 p.m. when Michael left, to 8 a.m. when my sister Diana or my mother arrived. The first one, Devon, was efficient and caring; I felt completely comfortable with her. Unfortunately, because of prior commitments, she only lasted for a few weeks.

Her replacement, Mary, was not as good. She stayed with me for almost one month. She was very nice to me, but I wasn't comfortable with her; she didn't seem very competent. Although she was a steady, living presence in my room, she was more like a potted plant than a nurse. Ditzy and not "all there," if you know what I mean. She wasn't of much use to me.

"Can you try to get me someone else?" I asked Michael one evening before he headed out.

A few days later, I was assigned a new nurse who was competent and friendly to me, but only stayed two nights. The next one was stern, with a very abrupt demeanor, like a nurse in the marines. I immediately nicknamed her

Nurse Ratched, after the dour, evil, blank-faced character brilliantly played by Louise Fletcher in the movie, *One Flew over the Cuckoo's Nest*.

She introduced herself to my brother as *Ms. Smith.* As Michael was giving her the details on my condition, he paused and in a friendly tone asked, "I'm sorry, what's your first name?"

She didn't return his smile. "You can call me Ms. Smith," she said in an icy tone. You might call what followed an "uncomfortable silence."

Before Michael left that night, he leaned over to me with a smile and asked, "Do you want me to get rid of her?"

I laughed. "No, I'll be OK," I responded. After letting one nurse go because she was dizzy and incompetent, and losing a few others because of their unavailability, I felt I could put up with a hard-ass that wanted to be called Ms. Smith, as long as she knew what she was doing.

Well, I made a wrong call on that one. The minute I was left alone with her, she really started giving me the creeps. Nurse Ratched was high-strung and impatient. She paced around the room. She banged things around. She seemed rough and—I was starting to think—a little unhinged.

I was still only 110 pounds, and needed to be handled carefully. With all my tubes and infections, there were certain procedures I was very used to and I was trying to demonstrate to her, in my hesitant way, how things were done. She put her hand up to convey that she was hearing none of it. Things would be done her way. Before I went to bed that first night she was on duty, she hooked the antibiotic IV line into my arm. Almost immediately, it began to burn. When I attempted to let her know that pain from the needle for the antibiotics was unusual, rather than try to remedy it, she argued with me.

"These are antibiotics, after all," she said in a 'know it all' way that was almost as painful as the IV line. "You need them to keep fighting off the infection." She wagged her finger at me as if I was a disobedient three year-old. Then she folded her arms and stared me down with her cold, blank eyes. She absolutely refused to accept the fact that I had been in the hospital for a long time and knew more about my own injuries and issues than she did.

My arm continued to burn and I was tempted to rip the IV right out. It was a good thing I didn't because I would have seriously hurt myself. I didn't have enough of a voice or the strength to argue with her.

Luckily for me, she eventually left the room and I was able to press the button for the hospital nurse. I didn't know how long Nurse Ratched would be out of the room, so when the staff nurse arrived, I began to cry. It was the quickest way I could convey something was terribly wrong.

She became concerned, "What's the matter, Joe?" she asked gently. I used what little voice I had left to tell her that the IV was burning my arm. The moment I got my point across, Nurse Ratched returned. She stood at the door ready for a showdown with the "intruding" nurse.

"He's been suffering long enough," the staff nurse told Ratched. "He doesn't need to be in any additional pain. Our job is to keep him as comfortable as possible." Nurse Ratched's eyes burned with fury—but she remained silent. Seething. She watched as the kind nurse efficiently diluted the antibiotics with water. It instantly felt better. I blew her a kiss.

"Goodnight," she said as she left me alone with wretched Ratched.

Needless to say, I didn't sleep well that night. Nurse Ratched, incensed now that her competency had been questioned, continued to bang around the room as noisily and obnoxiously as possible. I'm sure she was doing it on purpose. She acted like a woman possessed. She constantly checked all the machines I was hooked up to, all the while babbling to herself. It started out as a joke, but now I was beginning to think of horror movies where helpless victims were left alone with ominous killers who are there in the guise of help. Every time I opened my eyes to check on what Nurse Ratched was doing, she seemed to be looking at me at that exact moment. Maybe her eyes never left my face. It was a nightmare. I changed the subject in my mind and tried to think of other things. I was finally beginning to doze off when: "Time for your bed bath," Ms. Smith announced in a creepy mock sing-song voice. It was 5 a.m.

"No way," I said hoarsely. I tried to put up a brave front. I didn't want her to know how terrified I was of her by now. She had already proven that she was oblivious to my condition. On top of that, she was in a rush to get her duties done and finish her shift. Warning bells were going off like crazy. She might pull out one of my tubes or, worse yet, get water in the trachea tube. I didn't want her touching me. I let her know I wanted to see a doctor.

"Now, now," she said in a faux, compassionate voice. "There are no doctors on the floor right now. Just let me give you your bath and by the time I'm finished, there should be some around by then."

I was insistent. I would not let this monster near me. "Get me a doctor," I said in the strongest voice I could muster. She pierced me with a steely stare and left the room.

A doctor finally arrived. I wrote him a note pleading with him to get rid of the nurse. *I don't want her near me.*

He looked at me curiously. "Why?" he asked, with his head cocked to the side.

Tears came to my eyes again. I scribbled, "I am afraid of her." He understood that my fear was genuine. He went to talk to her.

After a few minutes, the doctor returned to inform me, "She will not bother you again. She won't even come into your room. She does, however, want to be paid for the evening, so she will sit outside of your door." That was fine with me. As long as she wasn't near me.

Still, I couldn't fall asleep with that demonic bitch outside my door. I figured by now she was ready to snap. I lay in bed wondering, *what the hell is going on!* I'm in a hospital, dammit. I shouldn't have to constantly worry about some incompetent nurses and doctors hurting me even more. In my opinion, the first hospital caused the majority of my problems, and although this location was better, it was not ideal.

About 6 a.m. the doctors came into my room while on their rounds. I wrote a note to the one who had helped me out earlier, "Thank you for getting rid of that psycho nurse for me."

He laughed and passed it around to the other doctors who also laughed; they may have been laughing at me. They probably thought I was the insane one for chasing away my own private duty nurse.

They didn't have to suffer at her hands or witness her scary behavior so I didn't care what they thought. I was just relieved that she was gone.

That day, I told my family I did not want or need a private duty nurse anymore. I would be fine pressing the call button on the bed and waiting for the nurse on duty to assist me. Since I had some interaction with the hospital nurses during the day, I knew they were gentle and compassionate.

I would much prefer having to wait a few minutes for a sane, sensitive nurse then spend each evening on the edge, wondering and worrying what horror might befall me at the hands of the sadistic Nurse Ratched.

Chapter 18

Man in the Mirror

Even though Nurse Ratched was gone, I still had to deal with Maureen, the physical therapist.

Maureen continued to be very tough with me—impersonal, gruff, without an ounce of sensitivity. She most definitely gave off the feeling that, to her, I was a job, not a person. To say I didn't enjoy working with her would be a huge understatement. However, since I was determined to do whatever it took to grow stronger, I buried my personal feelings for her and always did as she instructed. Eventually, I would learn she did have a heart buried under her stoic facade.

One day she took me out of my room and brought me to the rehabilitation room for my therapy session.

I remember her telling me, "We can get a great deal more done here than we can in your room." Also, she wanted me to stand in front of a mirror and see how my neck and body were twisted. She thought if I could see for myself how crooked I was, it would be easier for me to try and straighten myself out. My body had been improperly curved for such a long time it felt perfectly normal to me. I couldn't understand what she meant when she would tell me to straighten up, because I already felt straight.

According to the doctor's theory, the muscles on the right side of my neck were elongated and stretched and the muscles on the left side were shortened and tightened. Since they thought it was a muscular problem, the doctors felt I could voluntarily correct it.

When Maureen pulled the full length mirror in front of me and ordered, "Stand in front of it," I did as instructed.

Seeing myself in that condition for the first time, the shock hit me like a sucker punch. It wasn't the "me" I was familiar with looking back from the mirror. The last time I saw myself I was a young, healthy man who took time and care with my personal grooming. Diet and exercise were important to the person I was and I took pride in my appearance. The stranger staring back at me was emaciated and unkempt. The whole body and neck were severely twisted in opposite directions. There was an ugly scar on the neck from the first tracheotomy tube. The face, on this man, was wan, red and blotchy due to the lack of a normal diet, fresh air and sunshine. I looked for a long time at the man in the mirror, slowly trying to absorb that this was me now.

I had never worked harder with her than I did that day. I couldn't get the image of that scary imposter in the mirror—who I knew to be me—out of my mind. I had to do everything in my power to get rid of him and get my old self back. I mentally compared myself in my current state to the photos hanging in my room and I was deeply disturbed by the change in my appearance.

After the session, Maureen wheeled me into the hallway and left me there momentarily while she returned to the rehab room because she had forgotten something. Alone in the hallway, I allowed the feelings of hopelessness and despair to overtake me. I put my head down and began to cry. Softly at first but it soon turned to loud, heaving sobs—tears poured from my eyes in buckets. Nothing had prepared me for the fact that I now looked so hideous. I couldn't understand how my family and friends would look at me and tell me how good I was looking. As compared to what? I wondered, *could I have looked any worse than this?* At that moment, I couldn't imagine it was even possible.

Maureen returned to see me crying, "Joe, why are you so upset?" she asked.

I was hysterical at that point so I had to spell it out in words. "So much," I managed to write. My appearance was awful, and I had so much to do to reverse all the damage. For the first time, something in me touched Maureen and she softened. Somehow, she understood what I meant and tried to console me.

"You'll do fine," she said encouragingly. "You're young, healthy, and have a very supportive family behind you."

Although I appreciated the fact that she at last saw me as a suffering human and was making an attempt to console me, I didn't really feel much better. When I finally composed myself enough to speak, I whispered, "I'll be okay." She nodded and silently wheeled me back to my room. Once there, I started to cry again.

After some time had passed, I have no idea how much, Diana arrived. I guess I had been sobbing for quite a long time and was in quite a state. My sister was alarmed. "Joe," she said gently, "What's the matter? What happened?" I spelled out the words "mirror." I could tell by the look on her face she understood. She realized I had finally seen what I looked like now. After some time I was able to stop the flow of tears. I could not, however, get the picture out of my mind of the freak that the accident had turned me into.

Chapter 19

Eating and Walking: Back to Basics

Through all the darkness there was always a little beam of sunshine that found its way to me and gave me another little push of encouragement. On the basis that my vocal cords were starting to function again, the doctors decided it was time for me to retake the "swallow test" (another video fluoroscopy). I was escorted to the radiation center where they stationed my wheelchair next to the X-ray machine. When I arrived there, I was handed a thick, milky substance to drink. It looked something like a milkshake, but tasted more like chalk. As I swallowed, the video X-ray showed the liquid as it traveled down my throat. The screen was directly in front of me so I was able to watch the entire process. I wasn't sure what I was looking for, but I did experience that peculiar feeling of watching the inside of your own body as if it were some kind of movie set for a science fiction film. After I took my first gulp, the technician added some water to the mixture. The moment I took another sip of the drink, he stopped the test.

The doctors reviewed the results and noted that although I handled the thick substance relatively well, I was unable to properly swallow any thinner liquids. One of them informed me, "Foods such as yogurt and pudding are fine, but you aren't ready for anything else."

I hadn't known this before, but the thicker a food or drink is, the easier it is to control and the thinner it is, the harder to control in your throat. Water is the hardest substance to control for anyone with swallowing problems.

The next morning some yogurt was brought to my room. Diana was with me, and I was nervous since I hadn't eaten real food in almost four months. Just the sight of food in front of me seemed strange and a little intimidating. The thought of eating it was even more unusual. I was uncertain if I would be able to chew and swallow it and it suddenly occurred to me that I was like a small child having my first try at solid food.

I took my first bite and simply enjoyed the feeling of the cool soft yogurt in my mouth. I chewed some, and then swallowed. Diana was watching me carefully, ready to jump into action if I started coughing or choking. After my first swallow, we looked at each other and smiled. I did it!

It was a wonderful feeling knowing that I could finally start eating again—another baby step towards returning to normalcy.

It only took a few days for me to become more comfortable with eating. It felt pleasant and refreshing in my mouth and throat; I was able to eat about four yogurts and three puddings daily. I was still also using the feeding tube to get all my calories and nutrients. But it felt wonderful to be able to contribute to increasing my body weight on my own. And, after such a long time away from flavor, food never tasted so good.

My ability to walk was also improving; I was able to take a few steps with Sandy's help. After doing this for a few weeks, I managed to get out of bed on my own by holding onto the wheelchair for leverage. I would make sure it was beside my bed at all times so I could stand up and sit down on it whenever I wanted. Being able to get out of bed and into the wheelchair on my own was a huge step towards some independence. I was elated and felt so free. I could sit down and read a book, call someone or write a letter. I felt like a king who had lost everything and was now given back a small amount of my power. I never, for a moment, forgot how much I had taken for granted before the accident, all the while keeping my focus on regaining the entire kingdom.

Chapter 20

Ready for Rehab

During the duration of my time at Cornell Hospital, Michael was trying to have me transferred to a rehabilitation center called Rusk, which is part of New York University in New York City. It has a reputation for being one of the best rehab centers in the state. At first, they didn't want to accept me while my lungs were infected with pneumonia. After I had the operation which cleared up the infection, they didn't want me because of the chest tube. I didn't understand their decision, but frankly, I didn't question it because it didn't matter that much to me. Michael, on the other hand, kept pushing to get me accepted.

Even though I couldn't comprehend the reasons why Rusk didn't want to accept me as a patient, I must admit I wasn't exactly upset with their rejection. I couldn't completely explain it then, but every time Michael mentioned the possibility of being moved to Rusk, I felt uneasy and I felt a tiny tremor below the surface of my emotions. First of all, I never heard of the place and had no idea of what to expect there. Even the name of it,

"Rusk," brought to mind a dark, gloomy sanatorium with stone walls and bars on the windows—filled with Nurse Ratcheds and God knows what else. Of course, now I understand the main reason for my apprehension. Today, I've learned about "comfort zones" and how the familiar always seems preferable to the unknown. I knew the people at Cornell and although it wasn't always ideal, at the very least, it was familiar. I felt safe.

Regardless of my fears of leaving Cornell, on March 29, around 11 a.m., one of the hospital nurses rushed into my room, exclaiming excitedly, "Rusk has accepted you, but you need to be there by 2 p.m. today."

Diana was with me and we looked at each other in surprise. I thought, *she must be kidding. All this time they wouldn't accept me, and now I had to get there with only a few hours notice?* Since the nurse didn't give us any indication she was joking, I realized it was true. Although, all my bottled up uncertainty about the place was causing me to tremble fully from head to toe, I knew it was in my best interest to go. It was time to move on. I immediately requested to see all the doctors, nurses, and therapists I had worked with during my time at Cornell. I wanted to thank them and say goodbye. Diana and I did our best to pack everything as fast as we could. Even though it was a hospital room, you'd be surprised at the things you amass over a period of months with family and friends looking after you. Diana then called a transport service to take me and the wheelchair. Within one hour, we were on our way.

My previous feelings of nervousness were gone by the time I left my room at Cornell. After we packed and were waiting for transportation, I became less afraid with every passing moment. Ever since I recovered from the chest operation, I was ready to move forward and, in spite of my fear of what was out there, I realized I needed a change. Before I had too much time to think about it, I was being wheeled directly from the sterile hospital into the transport van. This was the first time I had been outside in four months. An involuntary grin spread across my face as I experienced anew the beautiful feeling of fresh wind blowing across my face.

My eyes were wide with wonderment and excitement during the entire twenty minute long ride. For the first time in many months, although it seemed like years, I was able to see cars, buildings, and *people*. It felt strange to be out of the hospital, watching others driving, walking, talking and working.

I felt like a mole coming out of hiding, or an escaped convict feeling the sun after twenty years of hard time.

At one point, we hit some traffic, and I thought it was absolutely wonderful. After all I had been through and the months of monotony, I was truly happy that I could sit up and actually see, hear and experience the traffic. Wonderful traffic! Marvelous noise! Amazing visuals! I felt like a long deprived kid in a particularly well-stocked candy store. Prior to the accident, every single time I'd been stuck in a long line of cars, it irritated me. This time, however, I was able to enjoy and embrace the cacophony of life. *How good to be alive!* I thought, as a police siren wailed past us.

Upon arriving, my sister had to fill out all the tedious insurance forms and admission papers, as well as answer the expected questions. How frustrating it is to be thought of as a series of forms while your mind is screaming, *hey you! I'm a person!* After about a half an hour, which seemed like an eternity, we were led to my room. This place looked a lot like Cornell Hospital, but with one major difference. To my absolute delight, all of the patients were dressed in their street clothes instead of hospital gowns. I knew at once that I would feel more like a real person out of hospital garb, wearing my regular clothes every day.

As you could probably guess, after the big rush for me to get there within three hours, they were not prepared for me in any way, shape or form. Once we were in my new room, Diana and I noticed at once that, although there was a bed, there was no equipment set up. I'd just come from a room filled with beeping and humming sounds from all the machines that were necessary to sustain me. Diana started asking for my necessary equipment. At the time, I still needed three machines. I needed a feeding machine because I most certainly couldn't afford to lose any more weight. I needed a humidifier because without it my throat got painfully dry and would cause me to cough incessantly and a suction machine was essential because I still needed to be suctioned every so often.

In time, the staff started wheeling in the various equipment. But I didn't feel any safer. I was acutely nervous watching these nurses try to hook up the suction machine. It seemed as if no one there had ever done it or used one before.

After a few long hours, I had all three machines working and right next to my bed as I was used to having. It was somewhat comforting, but still not familiar.

Diana left at about 6 p.m. and my brother's girlfriend, Diane, showed up shortly after. I don't recall much about the first night, except, as it got later I started to feel lonely and unsure. I knew Diane would be leaving eventually and I wouldn't know anyone else. After being in Cornell for so long, I was friendly with all the nurses, aides, doctors and my roommates. I felt as if they were a support system, an extended family in many ways. Now, I felt like the new kid on the block. I might have been able to manage that if I was able to turn on the big personality and charm, but I was still very weak. Being new is hard enough under normal conditions, but not having all my full resources made the experience frightening. Think of the first day of school for an awkward child.

As the minutes ticked away, I could tell Diane was trying to console me and cheer me up. She had an "everything is going to be alright" demeanor, but I could sense that she was also uncertain and afraid. She stayed with me until about 9 p.m. when my brother came to pick her up. I really wished he was coming to pick us both up. After the long, exhausting day filled with so many mixed emotions, I cherished the idea of going home! I desperately wanted to get out of there.

But there's always a saving grace. For me, the saving grace that first night at Rusk was a nurse named Veronica. She was so sweet and understanding. She had an easy and casual manor and a good sense of humor that made me laugh. "Welcome to the Taj Mahal," she joked. She understood my situation. I relaxed.

Just as I was about to fall asleep, I became aware of a missing necessity. "Can I have a bedpan," I asked Veronica.

She chuckled. "When you need to use the restroom, just beep the nurses' station and an aide will come to assist you."

It seems like a little thing, but to me, at the time, this was huge—a major step. This was heaven to me. I fell asleep thinking how great it would be to never use a bedpan again.

At about midnight, I pressed the button to alert the nurses' station. Miracle of miracles! The aide came in, just as promised, and helped me get out of bed and led me to the bathroom. This was the first time in four months I didn't have to use a bedpan. Already, I was starting to feel more like a real human being again, and less like a sick person. It made me feel like I was finally winning the battle to become myself again.

Chapter 21

A Taste of Freedom

The first few days at Rusk are a bit of a blur; I don't remember much about the details of getting settled in. I met all my new doctors, nurses, and therapists. I was set up on a schedule for physical and occupational therapy; twice a day for each one. I can say that once I became comfortable with my new surroundings, I felt very optimistic and excited and, well, good! I most definitely enjoyed the fact I had more freedom here than in Cornell. The most joyous and hopeful part was that I was out of my room for most of the morning and part of the afternoon.

We are all used to living and following routines. My life now revolved around my new rehabilitation schedule. On a typical day, I would wake up around 7 a.m. The aides were available to assist me in getting dressed. Their help was essential, especially in the first few weeks. Breakfast arrived around 8 a.m. and consisted of my usual, yogurt and pudding.

At 9 a.m. I got into my wheelchair, wheeled myself to the elevator, and took it up to the second floor for therapy. Once there, a cozy feeling heating pad was placed on my neck for an hour which helped to relax my muscles and get them ready to work. Then Susan, my new physical therapist, would do some stretching exercises with me to try and straighten my neck and get some movement back in those muscles. She didn't want to be too aggressive since I still had the trachea tube in my throat, but we worked the best we could under the circumstances.

Afterward, I would have occupational therapy. We worked less on strength training and more on fine tuning tasks such as writing, typing, and sharpening my thinking skills. My occupational therapist, David, was a student intern and, over time, we became good friends. He was close to my age, which, in all my time at the three hospitals, was a rare find. He also hadn't been at Rusk very long and it didn't seem like he was part of the staff.

We played board games that required thinking, concentration, and memory. Sometimes we laughed so much during the games, it didn't feel like therapy. After months of concentrating only on survival, it felt so frivolous and enjoyable to simply concentrate on fun.

Joey Parenti is one of the greatest teachers I ever had and much of what I have achieved as a professional, I can attribute to his influence on me. It was not easy for him. It was frustrating and reminded him of all he had lost in the accident. But he wanted more challenges. He was determined to succeed. **David L, Occupational Therapist, Los Angeles, CA.**

One day, David wanted to work on my eye hand coordination, so he suggested we play knock hockey. This game has a wooden board that you lean over and try to knock the "puck" into your opponent's side. It's similar to air hockey, without the air. First one to get three points wins. You can't imagine how incredibly happy I was when I won the game!

He had this disappointed look on his face when he said, "Wow, I didn't even let you win!" It was a small victory, but at the time, I felt like I as if I had just won a gold medal.

After occupational therapy, I would return to my room for one hour to eat lunch which consisted of the same type of yogurt and pudding I'd eaten at breakfast. I'm not complaining. At the time, it still tasted great to me after so many months of nothing. After lunch was over, it was time to return to another session of occupational therapy and then physical therapy. The occupational therapy was pretty much the same in the afternoon, but physical therapy was much different.

During the afternoon session of physical therapy, I worked on standing and walking. I was pretty good at standing, and I could even work my way up from a sitting position to standing without much help. I was able to stay standing for a few minutes, and I was also able to sit back down on my own. It all felt exciting and new again to me, although it was routine for others. As something most people take for granted, let me assure you that after four months of lying in a bed, the feeling of accomplishment of being able to stand up again on my own gave me the same exhilaration as if I'd climbed Mt. Everest.

Much to my chagrin, walking was much more difficult. For the first week, I tried walking with an aide along each side of me. They held my arms and assisted me along with each painstaking step. That didn't work at all since my legs were still not strong enough. My therapist decided I should try a walker.

The idea was repugnant to me at first. I didn't want to do it because the connotation of a walker screamed "old person" to me. My mind still told me that I was a vital, young person. But my body told me otherwise. I had no choice. I gave in and used the walker.

What made this therapy so strange was how I had to actually think about walking. I would concentrate on my right foot, then the left foot. I had to tell myself, *don't drag the left foot. Hold your head up. Look in front of yourself. Pick up the walker, and do it again.* Trying to retrain all the muscles and think about each movement was extremely difficult for me. It was not something I ever had to do before. Like most people, before the accident I could get up, walk to another room while speaking to someone else, and return to my seat without an ounce of effort or thought. Now it took all my focus and concentration for me to walk a measly three steps. I sound like I'm complaining. And I am. At the time it was hell. But now I realize it was worth it because with every new step I took, it gave me a sense of pride and accomplishment. Of course, there were no awards or prizes, but I silently felt as if I earned one every time I went a little further.

Three weeks of the walker was enough for me. I then felt as if I was ready to try walking with two aides flanking my sides. My legs were getting stronger and my balance was better, so I was able to walk with their help. After about one week of assistance with two aides, I was able to take a few steps with only one aide. I was doing so well, that before long I managed to walk behind my wheelchair by holding on and pushing it. That worked out well, because once I got tired, which happened rather quickly, I was able to sit down and take a break.

Since the frontal lobe of my brain had been hit and damaged in the accident, I needed to do a great deal of work in occupational therapy to improve my coordination, memory, and hand movements. While my long term memory seemed fine, my short term was not. I easily remembered my name, where I lived, and all my friends and family by name. However, I had trouble recalling anything that occurred right before or even since the accident. If I asked a doctor or nurse a question and they answered it one day, I would often ask it again later in the day. I had no recollection of the fact that my question had been asked and answered earlier in the day.

Occupational therapy worked on that problem with reading comprehension tests similar to those in grammar school. I would read a story and then answer questions pertaining to it. This was very difficult for me, because I struggled to remember what I had just read. I could very much relate now to children with learning disabilities because that's exactly the situation I found myself in. It was very depressing. A few months earlier, I'd passed two parts of the CPA exam and graduated college. Now I'm at a 3rd grade reading level. Each time I tried and failed, my frustration rose. It was even more difficult to remember the story if my therapist read it to me. Reading the story made recalling the facts slightly easier than hearing the story read to me, but not that much easier.

To my great relief, it became a little easier for me as time went by. The hard work was paying off. When I learned to brush aside my frustrations and just keep focusing on the moment, I realized I'd move a little further.

Vocational therapy began about three weeks into my stay at Rusk. My vocational therapist, Mark, a tall thin man with dark hair and thick glasses had the idea that it was still possible for me to return to my fledgling career in accounting. He gave me as many math problems as he could find, and with much effort and determination, I did rather well with these. It gave me the motivation to think, to hope, to aspire to go back to my chosen profession of accounting. I decided that I wanted to prepare to go back to my career and was hell-bent on preparing. I suggested we use my study guides for the CPA exam and asked my mother to bring them in for us to work with. Mark tested me on one of the chapters which I did very well on, and we were both ecstatic.

I began meeting with Mark twice a week so he could test me on additional chapters and to discuss my plans for returning to work. During one of our sessions he suggested, "When you do feel ready to return to work, you should start part-time, only three half days a week. When you feel comfortable, slowly increase to three full days and work your way up to full time, five days a week."

This was a difficult concept for me to accept, since previously, before the accident, I had considered a twenty-five hour work week in a restaurant part time. I was a hard worker by nature and I felt I could eventually handle a full time work load better than the vocational therapist thought. But I was humble enough by now to accept that only time would tell.

In the midst of all of this, I was also scheduled to meet with a speech therapist. After meeting with her only once, she decided we should wait before meeting again. Her reasoning for this was that once my trachea tube was removed, it would be easier for me to speak and therapy would be more productive. At this point, I still had to cover the hole of my trachea tube with my finger for it to be possible to talk.

By 4 p.m. therapy was over and I would return to my room. Dinner was served at 5 p.m., yogurt and pudding, as usual. In the early evening, I usually had a few visitors, including my family or friends, and sometimes both. My progress had made visiting a much more pleasant experience. It was fantastic to be able to sit in my wheelchair while I spent time with them. During all the months being laid up in bed at Cornell, I felt so helpless and hopeless being flat on my back while I tried to communicate with them. Now, it was possible to have short conversations with them, eye to eye. It most definitively made me feel less like an invalid and lifted my spirits.

Since I was so busy with therapy in the daytime, my mother and sister Diana were relieved of their obligation to stay with me and were able get back to their lives. My mom went back to her full time job and my sister went back to being a full time mom. I was so grateful for the amount of time they sacrificed to care for me. I am sure the days were long and stressful for them. Now, for the first time in months, as my health improved, and I was becoming more independent, they were able to take their own lives and obligations into consideration. They continued to visit me whenever they had a spare moment—and always on weekends.

Michael was also relieved of his nightly duties and was able to start working a full day again. He continued, however, to visit a few nights a week with some friends.

Lily came to visit a few times, but on one of those visits she told me that she had gotten back together with an ex-boyfriend. I guess it was inevitable. She was a young, beautiful woman and we really didn't know each other very well or for very long before the accident. Of course, I was disappointed at the thought of losing her before I really had a chance to win her over. But, the reality of it was we had only dated a couple of times, and it was incredibly kind of her to visit me at all. More than anything, I could never forget or underestimate the magic of her kiss. The incredibly healing kiss she gave me, in spite of what I looked like and the condition I was in. That was a real gift that I couldn't possibly put a price tag on. I am forever grateful to that sweet soul.

I was also grateful for the freedom of being able to get into my wheelchair and use it on my own. I kept it beside my bed and enjoyed the comfortable cushions on the seat and back. Once I was in my wheelchair, I could go anywhere in the hospital by myself. This included the cafeteria, which was on my floor, or the main floor, where there was a candy store, a big luncheon, and a lounge with a sitting area and doors to the outside. I was no longer a prisoner.

One night, I wheeled myself to the elevator and rode it down to the main floor. I made my way to the lounge and sat close to the doorway, feeling the breeze and listening to the sounds outside. I guess I seemed very far away and eventually one of the visitors, a stranger to me, asked, "Do you need help?"

"No, I'm fine." I replied without hesitation. And I really meant it. I had spent so much time stuck in a small room in a hospital bed. Here I was, sitting by a doorway and breathing fresh air. With each deep breath I took, I felt more grateful to be alive. I was invigorated. I was reborn. For as long as I could remember, freedom was just something I took for granted. I never realized what a privilege it was until I lost it...shut away and confined. I was confident that I would eventually experience it again and even more sure that I would never again take it for granted.

Chapter 22

Losing the Chest Tube

Although there were moments of enjoying my new freedom, there were also many hours of lying around trying to remain optimistic and fill an empty feeling that would overtake me. It felt like hours of nothingness. I was always waiting for some new development that might signal I was a bit closer to recovery.

One evening, as I lay in bed experiencing a big dose of nothingness, a blonde, mustached, male nurse named Thomas came to my room to examine the surgical tape that covered my chest tube. This tube remained in place after the operation to drain any remaining fluid from my lungs. The tape had been on my chest for three weeks, so it had pretty much melded into my skin by this point. He looked at it carefully.

"I don't think you need all this tape here." Thomas said, "The chest tube was stitched into your skin during the operation and will hold fine on its own."

Since the incision and tape was on my left side, under my arm towards my back, I couldn't see what he was talking about. But I did know that the tape was starting to irritate me. I decided to trust his observation and allowed him to remove most of it. He reassured me that there were enough stitches and remaining tape to keep the tube in place.

A few days later, I was scheduled to get a CT scan of my chest. The nurses placed me on a cot, took me to a different floor of the hospital and left me there. When the X-ray technicians came, they wheeled me into the room and as they slid me from the cot to the CT scan machine, I felt a pull. My chest tube came right out...the chest tube that I'd been reassured would stay in place without the tape! I reached over to grab the tube, which was now completely out of my chest. I was trying to show it to the technicians, assuming they would know what to do with it. Well, they didn't. They had no idea where it came from or where it went. They thought it was hooked to me for urinating.

Since I still couldn't speak well, it was a real challenge trying to convey to them where it belonged. I kept shaking my head no, to indicate it didn't belong down there and pointed to the side of my chest. Finally, one of them realized what I was trying to say, and attempted to jam it back into my chest. This was an X-ray technician, not a doctor or even a nurse. He was like a plumber trying to fix an airplane with a plunger.

Annoyance turned to frustration which soon blossomed into full-fledged anger. Once again, I had put my trust in a "professional." Once again, I was let down. Although I understood there are always risks with any medical procedure, this incident made me realize that I really did need someone with me at all times. Someone I could trust. Someone who had my back. I had been so naive thinking that the safest place in the world for sick people is in the hospital. But, like everywhere else, mistakes can be made. And they are.

I had always viewed medical professionals as healing gods. But after this, and all my other bad experiences, I realized that no one in Rusk, or any other hospital for that matter, knew the extent of my injuries as well as I did. I was slowly and painfully learning that I had to be in charge of my own well-being. I had to be my own advocate. It was bad enough feeling so vulnerable all the time. This latest incident with the chest tube made me feel unsafe.

Eventually, the technician awkwardly managed to stick the tube back in my chest. The CT scan was taken and I was wheeled back to my room. I was still in a fury. I refused to go to therapy and demanded to see a chest surgeon.

A few hours later, the chest surgeon arrived and put the tube back in the proper place and taped it all up as it had been before.

A week later it fell out again, but this time it was decided it could be left out. That was a relief. I could check one more thing off the list of things I had to worry about.

But it left me with a painful reminder. That area on my chest never did completely heal. I was left with a large, unsightly scar and to this day, there are times when it is extremely painful. It feels like someone is grabbing my skin and squeezing it together—a torturous pinch. There's always discomfort there, but I've learned to live with it. Actually, I try to look to it as a reminder of how much worse it all could have turned out. It's always better to focus on the good rather than complain about the bad. Right?

Chapter 23

Don't Get Your Hopes Up

One morning in mid-April, my occupational therapist, David, informed me that the doctors had scheduled me for another "swallow test" the following day. David was becoming a good friend and he put his hand on my shoulder, "Don't get your hopes up, buddy" he warned me gently, "Your last test was very recent and it's unlikely there will be any improvement in such a short period of time."

I appreciated David's openness. I knew he was trying to protect me. He understood how disheartening the many weeks of false starts, misplaced hope and disappointments had been. By now, I knew the score. I needed to take everything one day at a time, to see how events unfolded—on their own terms and in their own time. Still, though, I couldn't help but feel a tinge of hope.

The next day, I wheeled myself to the exam room and met with David and the X-ray technician. Once I sat in the chair connected to the X-ray machine, I looked up and could see them in the next room through the glass window. They were watching a video screen similar to the one I had watched during this same test at Cornell. I knew the drill. They presented me with a thick milkshake. As I drank it, they carefully watched to see how my swallowing mechanism was working. The drink was then watered down the same way it was in my previous test. After I drank some more, they added more water. This went on two more times. I had no idea of how I was doing. They looked very serious as they watched the screen, pointing to it and talking to one another.

Their solemn, thoughtful expressions and in-depth discussion made me nervous. Soon my head was filled with worst case scenarios: *What if I haven't improved at all? What if I am destined to a diet of yogurt and pudding for the rest of my life?* This led me to thinking of all the delicious things I might never taste again.

Just as my mind was formulating a menu of the things I would miss most, David looked up flashing me a huge grin. Then he gave me the thumbs up sign. I smiled broadly. I couldn't help but feel triumphant, like a fighter who just won my toughest match yet. My swallowing had improved! I could almost taste all the food I'd been missing.

After the test, David explained to me, "You are now ready for what we refer to as mechanical soft foods and liquids." He continued, "Mushy items like pasta, bread, and cooked vegetables are good. That being said, you are not yet ready for dry food such as toast and crackers or fresh fruit and vegetables."

When I told my sister Lisa, the health expert, she didn't take the news as I expected. Actually, she was very upset. She claimed I needed the vitamins from the fruits and the vegetables to regain my strength as soon as possible. I listened to her lecture, but it didn't really sink in that much. At that moment, I was so happy to finally be able to expand my diet beyond pudding and yogurt that I wasn't concerned about missing any vitamins.

David sat with me the first few times I tried a new food. I was instructed to put only one food item in my mouth at a time and swallow one extra time after each bite. I needed two swallows to get each mouthful down because the muscles in my throat were still very weak. It felt strange at first and I was very nervous. Once again, it took a great deal of concentration and I had to go very slowly. I didn't let my mind wander while I was eating. I had to focus all my energy on the task at hand. It was odd for me to have to think about something I did so naturally for twenty-three years. I took my time, concentrated and eventually felt more and more comfortable eating.

In addition to the positive step of being able to eat again, the ENT doctor at Rusk, who I'd met once before and already liked more than Dr. Doom (which wasn't that difficult), gave me great news. He came to my room in the beginning of May to examine me and told me, "If you're careful, you can now take a shower."

It was such a delightful shock, I had to let it sink in for a moment. "W-what?" I asked.

He smiled back at me, "Yes, a shower, just be careful. The nurses will help you."

Memories of warm water soothing my aching body filled my mind. I was really excited; it had been over five months since I had taken a shower.

That evening, two female nurses helped me into a chair that was set up in the shower. Getting undressed and having them assist me in the shower was embarrassing, as you could imagine. However, in anticipation of a glorious, hot shower, I let go of my shyness. The hand held shower head was connected to a long cord. One of the nurses simply held it and pointed it to the parts of my body that she wanted to wash. She was exceptionally careful when washing my hair. She didn't want to get any water in the trachea tube, since it was a direct opening to my lungs and would have created additional problems.

After five months of bed baths, there are simply no words to describe just how wonderful that shower felt. As I was sitting there, enjoying the warm water and how great it felt on my skin, I was thinking how lucky I was to be alive. Amazing to think how in the past I'd jump in the shower every day and took for granted a ritual which was now a luxury.

Now that I was eating and showering, I started wondering when the trachea tube would be removed. I couldn't wait to get that awful, exasperating, painful thing out of my throat. Not only did it hurt, it also affected my sleeping. Breathing in the unfiltered air all day caused my throat to become very dry and irritated. Once I would lie down at night, I would begin coughing nonstop. I would always fall asleep easily, but kept waking up with a coughing fit. I never slept through the night and I'd wake up exhausted. This made my days more difficult, because the more tired I was, the harder it was to complete all my therapies. With so little energy, my recovery was taking much longer. When I complained about this to Dr. Shea, my primary doctor in Rusk, he offered me sleeping pills. I refused them without hesitation; I didn't want any more drugs in my system.

Thomas, the nurse, helped me solve this problem. At first, I was reluctant to accept his help since he was the one who took all the tape off my chest, causing the chest tube to fall out. But I was, well, desperate...and willing to give him another chance. He was able to make a makeshift plug for me that I could slip into the trachea tube. This blocked air or anything else from getting in. I eventually left it in all day. With the trachea tube covered, I didn't have to hold it in order to speak. The plug did it for me. I was able to leave it in all day and night. This was another incredible feeling for me. With each milestone, I felt increasingly better. Now I could eat, shower, walk with the wheelchair, and talk on my own. It was like winning the lottery!

I met with Dr. Shea and showed him the plug. "Since I'm able to breathe on my own with the trachea tube covered," I said, "when can it be removed?"

He responded, "It can't be removed until you stop needing the suction machine." He explained to me that I had to be able to clear my throat on my own. He could not remove the tube and close up the trachea until then.

This didn't make any sense to me. I thought one of the main reasons I was using the suction machine in the first place, was the tracheotomy tube in my throat. From what I understood, breathing in any unfiltered air directly into my throat caused mucus to build up. I thought I would stop using the machine once the trachea tube was removed and the hole was permanently closed up. He kept insisting that he could not remove the trachea tube until I stopped using the suction machine.

I had unfortunately learned there was no arguing with doctors. I decided the best way to move forward was to follow his advice and cut down using the machine and eventually stop using it at all.

From that point on, when I felt the need to be suctioned, I tried really hard to cough up what I could on my own and use the machine less. I wanted the trachea tube removed so I could go home. The strides I had been making provided perfect motivation. It was only five days after my first shower that I used that suction machine for the last time!

Chapter 24

Torture Test

The amount of tests the doctors took was really starting to put my patience to the test, but they were necessary. I was game. On May 20, Dr. Shea scheduled me for something that was called an Electromyography. This exam would determine if the nerves in my neck were sending impulses to the appropriate muscles. Since I had developed muscle atrophy on my right shoulder, the test was used to assess the corresponding nerves. Even though I had been through so many tests, I'd never heard of this particular test and didn't have a clue of what to expect.

By this point, as you could imagine, I was inured to pain. But nothing I had experienced before prepared me for what this particular test had in store for me. The neurologist, Dr. Lee, began the exam by sticking a needle into a specific location on my back. If you are thinking this procedure was something like acupuncture, remove that image from your mind. There was nothing gentle or refined about this. He proceeded to push the needle in deeper and then wiggle it around. Just when I thought the pain couldn't get more excruciating, he'd pull the needle out and stick it into a different spot. He did this at various places all over my back and, believe me, it felt like I was being tortured. If I had any secrets he was trying to get out of me, I would have gladly given them up. I closed my eyes, held my breath, and tried very hard to keep my composure. I attempted to take my mind off of it by thinking of other things—the beach, a dance club, a girl, the lyrics to a song—but this wasn't the kind of pain you could distract yourself from.

This went on for at least ten minutes. Just when I thought I couldn't stand it anymore, the doctor pointed out eight additional places he wanted to test. That was it. I lost it. I broke down...and started to cry. I cried because of the pain. I cried because I was tired of tests. And I cried because there wasn't an end in sight.

"No way," I said through my tears. "I can't take any more of this."

Dr. Lee could tell from my current state that I was in no condition to continue. He let me go back to my room.

A few days later, Dr. Shea mentioned that I should complete the test, "I can't stress how important it is," he stated. I didn't want to refuse any exam that could help me in my recovery, so I agreed. I felt I could give it another try.

At least now I knew what to expect. This time I spent hours beforehand trying to prepare myself for the ensuing pain. "If it gets too bad, you could always put a stop to it," I reassured myself. "People have been through much worse," I said aloud. Soon, I was again a human pin cushion in front of Dr. Lee. Fortunately, he completed the remainder of the test quickly. The pain still made me see stars and want to bite down on a bullet, but since I was prepared, it wasn't as bad as the first time.

The next day, Dr. Shea came to my room to give me the results of the exam. He explained how one of the nerves that connected my neck to my shoulder was injured and not doing its job of stimulating the muscle in my right shoulder, something called neurogenic atrophy. This created a loss of muscle mass and a winged scapula; my shoulder blade would pop out from my back when I tried to lift up my right arm.

It sounded serious, but so much of what happened to me was serious and I was glad it was finally diagnosed. "Okay. Good," I said with a smile. Now that we know what the problem is, how do we treat it?"

"Oh, there is no treatment for that," he stated matter-of-factly.

I was shocked at his reply and his blasé tone. I thought to myself, *are you kidding? This must be some kind of a joke. Why would you have me go through a test as painful as that...twice? Was it all to diagnose a problem that can't be fixed? Is that what you consider "Very important?"* At that time, I wasn't emotionally or verbally strong enough to say all that, but I couldn't stop thinking it. Why put a patient through a painful diagnostic test if there was no treatment available? I mean, I presume they needed to know for sure if I had neurogenic atrophy, but now that they had their answer and there was nothing they could do about it, the whole thing seemed cruel and pointless.

On a more positive note, or so I thought, the ENT doctor came to my room later that month to remove the trachea tube. He asked me to lean my head back slightly—which I did—and then without any warning he slowly pulled it out of my throat. It was rather disgusting. "We'll leave it open for a few days to see if this hole in your throat closes on its own."

Wow, I had really wanted that tube removed, but after he took it out, I didn't feel good about it at all. My throat was ghastly open, which made it impossible to speak, and I couldn't even plug it up to keep it clean. I came up with the idea of using some gauze to cover it. I feared that dust or water or God knows what else might get in there. Keeping it covered seemed like a logical thing to do and pretty simple. It baffled me that no doctor or nurse suggested it.

I struggled through the next few days having to cover this hole in my throat with my fingers while I spoke and kept it double covered while in the shower.

About a week later, the hole in my throat had not closed on its own and the ENT doctor scheduled the operation to close it.

I had mixed feelings about the whole thing. I mean, after five months with a hole in my throat, the idea of having it closed up was a great relief. But, on the other hand, I was really nervous about yet another surgery.

I pushed all my reservations aside as they put me on the cot and started the by now familiar procedure of hooking up the IV and anesthesia. I was knocked out pretty quickly. The operation went well, but the skin there looked red and raw. Today, I have many scars, little reminders, etched on my neck.

The night after the operation, I was exhausted. Still, I went to bed incredibly happy and hopeful. I slept fine for a few hours, but woke up in the middle of the night with a choking spasm. I was wheezing and gasping for breath.

It became so loud the nurses heard it from down the hall. In a matter of minutes, my bed was surrounded by doctors and nurses—gawking at me. But just as suddenly as the choking started, it stopped; the gaggle of medical professionals left my bedside and I fell back asleep.

The next morning, I was seen by the ENT doctor. He examined me again with the cord through my nose down into my throat (it did not get easier with time). "Everything is working fine," he announced. "I'm not sure what happened last night. The muscles in your throat may need more time to start working properly."

I didn't feel well that day so I stayed in my room and didn't go to any therapy. I thought that, perhaps, if I rested, if I gave myself a break from my daily routine, I would start to feel better. I didn't. Actually, I was feeling worse. All that day I was nauseous and dizzy. When the doctors came in on their evening rounds, I was anxious to tell them about my new symptoms. I rarely complained about anything in the past and I thought that would be a signal to them that I was serious. I thought they would act immediately. How wrong I was!

Dr. Shea looked at me and said, "It's probably just from the operation."

I was beat up and tired from not feeling well all day and I fell asleep soon afterwards. At 3 a.m. I woke up, leaned over the bed and vomited all over the floor. I was sick, dizzy, light-headed and delirious; like a case of alcohol poisoning.

The nurses once again heard me and rushed into my room. The doctor on call that night examined me and ordered blood tests to determine what was going on. The blood test showed that the medication I was taking to prevent seizures, Dylantin, had built up to toxic levels in my bloodstream. He ordered the medication to be stopped until I was examined by the neurologist.

The next day, when I told Michael about it, he reminded me, "In Cornell they took your blood often to monitor it. That's why this never happened there." But, he was quick to add, "Of course, it *did* happen in Jamaica Hospital."

Later that day, when I mentioned this to Dr. Shea, he replied, "Oh, we were monitoring it here as well. It must have shot up because of the recent operation."

I was incredulous. *How could they be monitoring it if not a single person drew my blood in all the time I'd been there?* But I said nothing.

The neurologist came into my room that evening and asked me, "Have you had a seizure yet?" I informed him I hadn't.

"OK, we're taking you off the Dylantin." He then nonchalantly stated, "If you have a seizure, let me know so we can put you back on it." Then he casually strolled out the door.

This was becoming surreal.

Even the nurse, who was in my room at the time, couldn't believe what she'd just heard. She walked over to me with a confused look on her face. "Did he just say what I think he did?"

Yes he did. There I was in a hospital with one doctor lying through his teeth about blood tests and another telling me to call him if I had a potentially fatal seizure. Nice.

Once again, I started replaying my entire experience. How danger lurked in every situation and how hospitals are hardly a safe haven to recuperate in. Just like the outside world, they were wrought with danger and incompetence. How many close calls and downright errors had I survived?

It didn't seem fair. It didn't seem right. I was coming from a work ethic where it was imperative that I always do the best job I possibly could. It was beyond my comprehension that professionals who worked in a field where human lives were at stake could seem at times so unconcerned, or even incompetent. At least, that's how I saw it at the time.

Chapter 25

One Step at a Time

In spite of the frustrations, anger and incompetence I experienced each day—in various different ways—I continued to take steps. Steps towards turning my situation around. I had begun to walk on my own, taking steps here and there, without holding on to the back of the wheelchair. I was improving, albeit slowly. It was difficult to walk with my head tilted to one side, but I was managing pretty well. My physical therapist, Susan, would walk by my side in case I stumbled—but my legs were getting stronger and my balance was getting better and better.

Susan also had me start working out on the leg machine. There were no weights on this machine, so the resistance was based upon how hard I pushed. If it was lightly, I got little resistance and vice versa. I began using this machine twenty minutes a day. My legs were definitely getting a bit stronger every time I used it.

By this time, I could walk as much as I wanted as long as the wheelchair was with me, in case I was too tired to walk back. It was such a great feeling. My head may have been tilted to one side and my balance somewhat off, but each time I made it to the end of the hallway, I felt like I'd won a marathon and I was ready to claim my title.

After a few days of pacing up and down the corridor without any assistance, one of the other physical therapists asked me, "Have you tried the stairs yet?"

Stairs? I hadn't even been thinking of stairs. I was happy to make it to the end of the hallway and back. "No, I haven't," I replied.

"Well, I've been watching you," she smiled, "And I think you're definitely ready for that."

Flushed with the feeling of accomplishment, I wanted to push myself further. "Okay," I replied with a smile.

We walked to the nearest staircase. "One step at a time," she encouraged. "I'll be right behind you."

I looked up the staircase. Some of my confidence flew the coop momentarily. I hadn't even seen a staircase in five months. I wasn't sure I still knew how to get up a flight.

I cautiously grabbed on to the railing and started up. Like a toddler trying the stairs for the first time, I had to put one foot on the first step, and then put the other foot on the same step. Deep breath. Then to the next. Luckily, I had some strength in my arm by this time, because I needed it to help pull me to the next level. Slowly but surely, I made it to the top. Whew!

The therapist beamed with me at my accomplishment. "Now," she said brightly, "Let's try going down." Um.

Down? I was happy enough going up. Going down looked much scarier. I looked at the bottom and momentarily imagined myself splattered on the floor.

I pushed that image away. *They're just steps, after all,* I told myself. *You've been going up and down them your entire life.* I took a deep breath and started down. I alternately lifted each foot and each time it felt unsteady. I wasn't sure it would land in the right place. It also made me realize how weak my legs still were. I was particularly nervous when stepping on to my left foot, which was my weaker side. With a lot of trepidation and anxiety, I eventually made it to the bottom of the staircase.

I must have been holding my breath on the way down. Once I reached the bottom, I exhaled deeply. I was elated. I started to giggle and then it turned into full-fledged laughter. It was the kind of laugh that mixed fear and elation. The therapist laughed with me. It was the most empowering moment I'd had since the accident.

A few days later, filled with pride and a new sense of self, I decided to walk from my room to physical therapy without having the protection of the wheelchair with me. Then, energized with confidence, I decided to take the stairs also. By myself! Sure I was a bit wobbly, a little uncertain...more than a little, but step by step, I accomplished it with no problem at all. This was another giant leap forward.

I couldn't wait to share my accomplishment with my occupational therapist. David, however, was not as joyful as I was. "What! You used the stairs by yourself?" he exclaimed. "Are you crazy? What if you fell? What if no one knew where you were?" David was usually a soft-spoken guy, but my "antics" really pissed him off. "Don't ever do that again!" He snapped.

I understood his concern, but I didn't let his agitated tone get to me. I was too busy basking in my accomplishment. For the next few days, David accompanied me when I climbed the staircase. Eventually, he was assured that I could go it alone.

Later that week someone mentioned to me that there were laundry machines on the 4th floor. I immediately made a plan to do my own wash from then on. I realize that, for most people, doing the laundry is not something that is noteworthy in any way. It's mundane at best and an annoying, tedious chore at worst. But I felt joyous every time I did the wash. I was a little more independent. A little freer. Another step closer to taking charge of my own life again.

Chapter 26

Are You Going to Eat That?

Near the end of May, almost six months since the accident, Dr. Shea walked into my room one morning, with a cheerful air. "You can now have a day pass if you want to leave the hospital for a few hours," he declared, "as long as someone is with you."

I had to let that sink in for a minute. It sounded too good to be true. I cleared my throat. "Excuse me?"

He laughed, "Yes, you can leave…just make sure you come back."

I felt like I might spring up and start to dance. I immediately called my brother and we started making plans for my first outing.

The next Saturday, Michael came to pick me up and drove me to my parent's house in Howard Beach. Being in the car with him, driving away from the hospital, felt like there should be a Disney soundtrack playing in the background. It was a dream come true. I knew it was only going to be for a few hours, but it still meant the world to me.

It was Mother's Day weekend and we wanted to surprise my mom. We parked, got out of the car, and I walked to the front door by myself. I rang the doorbell. My mom answered and screamed with surprise and joy. For a minute, I thought she might faint.

It was an odd mixture of old and new—familiarity with wonderment. It was odd to be in a "normal" environment after six months in hospital settings. But it was the house I grew up in, the most comfortable place in the world to me.

I spent the day eating my mom's amazing cooking and just relaxing—enjoying the normalcy of it all.

In the evening, I went back to my apartment with my brother, a few friends and my niece, DeNina. It all felt surreal, like I was watching a movie about someone else who was a stranger, but also very familiar. This was another huge step towards knowing I was going to have a normal life again, eventually.

One day, near the end of May, I was able to use the day pass to go to my cousin's wedding in New Jersey. My brother came to pick me up at the hospital and brought one of my suits from home. As I walked out of my hospital room, all the nurses started whistling and clapping. It felt so great, especially knowing that when I first got there, two months earlier, this would have been totally impossible.

He drove us to the wedding and it was wonderful to see my aunts, uncles and cousins. They were treating me like a celebrity. Everyone wanted to talk to me. They all kept telling me how great I looked. I remember feeling very fortunate and loved.

I mentioned to my sister Diana that I thought one of the girls there was cute. After Diana went over and spoke with her, the girl came over and danced with me. Dancing with her was amazing and brought back such wonderful memories.

It was so much fun. I'm fairly certain I didn't look all that great dancing, but I wasn't self-conscious or inhibited. I was free! Free! Utterly free!

I knew it would be a long day, so I brought the wheelchair with me. As we were leaving, I was holding on to the wheelchair for support and pushing it in front of me. When I walked past the girl I had danced with, she pointed to the wheelchair and said, "I don't think you need that anymore." And I thought, w*ow, it's really great to be alive!*

The next weekend, my sister Lisa was graduating from chiropractic school in Georgia. My whole family went to see her, but unfortunately, I couldn't join them. I was totally bummed. I had a pass to go out, but nowhere to go.

Luckily for me, my friend Denise from BDO Seidman came to visit that night. I was happy to see her and said, "I have a pass. Let's go out for dinner." She seemed reluctant. As I think back now, she probably didn't want to be responsible for me.

But I didn't want to waste a pass, so I kept on insisting until she gave in. We started walking to a Chinese restaurant that was only two blocks away. There was a comfortable breeze and I noticed how it blew through her long, honey-blonde hair.

As we were walking, she touched my arm lightly and said, "Joe it's so amazing that you can actually leave the hospital now. I can't even imagine how difficult all these months have been for you."

"Thanks Denise, it's been a nightmare," I responded. I thought about the last few months. Suddenly, a picture of the doctor sticking needles in my back came to me. "It's been something like Chinese water torture, slow and painful," I added with a frown.

When we arrived at the restaurant, it was packed with a weekend crowd. There was only one table available in the middle of the restaurant. It was a table for four. I sat with my back to the kitchen and Denise sat across from me with the bar and restrooms behind her. Our food arrived and soon we were eating and chatting comfortably. At one point, I noticed Denise looking at me with a sparkling smile.

"What are you thinking about?" I asked. "Please share, I could use a good laugh."

"Well," she said, as I took a forkful of food, "I think it's a little bit ironic that after going through a type of Chinese torture, you'd be craving Chinese food."

I still had some food in my mouth, but I couldn't help myself, I started laughing. On my next inhale, a piece of rice blocked my windpipe for a second and then another choking spasm happened.

Denise saw me struggling for air and asked, "Are you okay?" As I was wheezing, I shook my head no. "Can somebody help me?" she screamed. "Does anyone know the Heimlich maneuver?"

Denise later told me: "I was watching you turn blue…I was watching this poor guy, who just endured almost six months of hell in a hospital, die while having a meal with me. It may have only been a few seconds, but it felt like an eternity to me."

I continued straining to breathe. Each time I did, I got louder. I started to think, *it's a good thing we are so close to the hospital. I think I'm going back there and they'll have to reopen the trachea.*

That isn't what happened. There were people all around the table and one of them was yelling. The cook, a really huge Chinese guy, came out from the kitchen and gave me the Heimlich maneuver. It felt like he was going to break another rib. I stopped wheezing and managed to say, "It's not food." I didn't think it was a food blockage since this happened before without food. But, maybe it was food because after the Heimlich, I was able to breathe normally.

I think there were a few doctors and nurses there since a few of the customers around the table were asking me questions. One inquired, "Do you have asthma?" Another yelled out, "Do you have a trachea problem?" I nodded yes, and gave her a thumbs up. When I looked up at last, I saw my poor friend Denise sitting there crying. I felt really awful since I was the one who insisted we go out to dinner and then proceeded to almost choke to death in front of her.

I felt horrible and I gave her a heartfelt apology for putting her through that. We were both frazzled and discombobulated by the entire experience and just sat there quietly for a few moments trying to collect ourselves.

Then the will for normalcy came over me again. I looked at Denise. Then I looked at her plate and pointed, "Are you going to eat that?" I asked. She pushed the dish over to me. Although my choking fit had caused a scene, I was still hungry and wanted to enjoy non-hospital food as much as possible.

When I couldn't eat another bite, the waitress came to the table with the bill. She asked if we wanted the remainder of the food wrapped to go. Denise seemed irritated. She gave the waitress an annoyed look, as if to say, *you've got to be kidding me.*

I had fully recovered from my choking ordeal now and thought it was a great idea, "Sure, thank you."

Denise treated me to the dinner. I know she felt horrible about the entire experience. She later told me, she was so traumatized she took a CPR class a few weeks later to learn the Heimlich maneuver. She never wanted to be in that position again.

I, on the other hand, was used to these minor emergencies, and bounced back from it quickly. Still, on the walk back to the hospital we were both pretty quiet. She left shortly after we arrived back at my room.

After Denise was gone, I described the events of the evening to one of the nurses. She decided to sit with me while I finished the remainder of the food from the restaurant. Her concern was that I might be so traumatized by what happened that I might be afraid to eat again or maybe even stop eating altogether. That wasn't the case at all. Appetite intact, I finished eating everything without any problems.

The next day, I told David the entire story. "How about you stay away from rice for a long time?" He suggested. "And refrain from speaking when eating while you're at it." Then he winked at me.

I agreed. Although the event at the restaurant had rattled Denise to the core, I was strangely unaffected by it. What was one more near death experience after six months of being on the Grim Reaper's doorstep?

·

In my apartment – almost 6 months after the accident

Chapter 27

Six Long Months

One morning, in the beginning of June, I was in physical therapy with the hot pack around my neck when I suddenly began to miss my old life more intensely than usual. All at once, I became consumed with an intense fury. I was sick and tired of living in hospitals and felt gloomy and homesick. The emotional pain was so bad it actually felt physical. I attempted to wheel myself into the corner, because I knew the tears were about to spill.

I found an empty area of the therapy room and let it out. The past few months of pain and suffering had gotten to me. I had been holding it in for so long while working hard to get better. I was worn down and I just fell apart emotionally.

When one of my physical therapists, Katie, got word of where I was and the state I was in, she offered to take me outside for some air. Once I felt the sun's rays on my face, I calmed down a bit. Katie was very sweet and would sometimes teasingly imitate the way my neck was twisted by tilting her own head. She did it now. Normally, I would smile in appreciation. This time I just stared at her.

"What's bothering you today?" she asked

"I want to go home," I said simply.

She tried to reason with me and explain why being at Rusk was better for me. I heard the words, but they were not sinking in. All I could do was tell her that I needed to go home. I could not stay there anymore.

It was clear to her my mind was made up. "When do you want to go home?"

Without hesitation, I responded, "Today." She laughed and told me if we set a reasonable goal we could work toward it. I thought about setting a realistic goal. I told her my birthday was in three weeks, and I would really love to be home by then.

"Okay, then we'll work on it," Katie replied.

Lunch was served at noon and I just couldn't eat. I started to cry again. Mary, one of the nurses, tried to console me. "My brother went through something similar. These things take time." She was doing her best to comfort me and I appreciated it, but I was still upset. I had gone way beyond the point of consoling words. I just wanted my old life back.

About 4 p.m., it became clear to me what was going on. As I looked at the calendar, I read the date, June 5th. It was exactly six months since my accident. As odd as it sounds now, I believe in the recesses of my mind I sensed that, and was reacting. My subconscious was grieving half a year of my life wasted—spent in pain and turmoil.

Katie fulfilled her promise and spoke to Dr. Shea. A few days later, he came to see me, "I'm going to grant you your birthday wish," he said, "You will be home for your birthday."

He told me my discharge date would be on June 28, two days before my birthday. I couldn't believe it was actually going to happen...I was thrilled! I felt as though I had been in prison for six months.

I immediately started calling everyone to tell them the great news. I first called my parents, brothers and sisters. Then I started calling all my friends. I think I said the same thing to everyone I spoke to, "Guess what? I'm coming home!" I spent the whole afternoon on the phone enjoying the conversations and hearing how happy they were for me. Once again, the feeling of being truly loved was a balm.

For the next three weeks, I worked exceptionally hard at walking, standing, sitting and everything else I could think of to prepare me for starting back in the real world. I was more motivated than ever before because I knew I would soon be free.

To prepare for my discharge, Dr. Shea wanted me to spend one night in a room off the main floor to be sure I would be comfortable without the nurses or aides assistance. I was allowed to have one person stay with me. I, of course, asked Michael if he could sleep overnight at the hospital. He agreed and we scheduled this two days before my discharge.

It was a small, sparse room with two beds and a television set. Michael and I watched TV and briefly discussed my imminent freedom. While we were watching TV, I fell asleep. I slept peacefully for a few hours, but woke up at about 3 a.m. having a minor choking spasm. This was the third time I'd had one, so the fierce panic didn't overtake me. I remained calm and lulled myself into breathing normally.

Michael woke up, looked over at me and asked, "Are you OK?"

"Yes," I replied confidently.

"OK, good," Michael said as he rolled over and fell back asleep.

I was also able to fall asleep after a few minutes.

The next morning, when the nurse asked me how my night was, I was reluctant to tell her about my choking spasm. I didn't want Dr. Shea to have any second thoughts about my discharge.

I replied, "It was fine. I did wake up coughing, but it didn't last long." I knew if I'd said "choking" instead of "coughing," it would've sounded worse even though that more accurately described what happened

Maybe I should've been more honest, but I was ready to go home.

Chapter 28

Going Home

On June 28th, almost seven months after the night of my accident, my sister Diana came to pick me up. We packed everything, and I spent some time saying my goodbyes to the nurses, doctors, and aides. After three months of being in Rusk, I was friendly with everyone, and I wanted to thank them for all their help and support. It felt very strange as we got into Diana's car. The long and near impossible battle was finally over.

She drove from Rusk in New York City directly to Uno's Pizzeria in Forest Hills, NY, which used to be my favorite place to eat. She wanted to treat me to lunch before taking me home. I ordered a chicken cutlet sandwich and it was the best sandwich I had ever eaten, because I was finally free!

A few days later, my friend Anthony called and invited me over for a visit to take a dip in his pool. He picked me up from my apartment and told me we had to pick up my brother Michael from my parent's house.

As we turned the corner on my parent's block, I started to hear loud screaming coming from their front yard. I tried to turn my head to see what the commotion was, but really couldn't see because of my stiff neck. Once Anthony stopped, and I got out of his car, I could not believe my eyes. My entire front yard was filled with about forty of my friends and family.

"Surprise!" the crowd shouted from the front lawn. A big white banner hung on the front of the house that read "Welcome Home JP!"

In the local paper there was a half page announcement that read: "Welcome Home, Joseph Parenti, On Your 24th Birthday From All Of Us Who Love And Have Missed You!"

I was overcome with emotions. Tears filled my eyes. The sheer amount of love I felt from everyone moved me more than I ever thought possible. I had just dealt with the most traumatic experience in my life, but all of these people were behind me every step of the way. I know now I couldn't have made it through that ordeal without them.

I thought the joy everyone felt was similar to when parents bring a newborn home. The difference with this celebration was that I wasn't new to the world. I'd already seen and lived through so much in my life. However, I knew I would see it with fresh, grateful eyes from this point on.

Sometimes we have to die before we learn how to live.

Welcome Home Party

Conclusion

As I write this now, I am forty-nine years old. It has been twenty-six years since my accident. My total confinement was just under seven months, twenty-nine weeks to be exact, in three different hospitals.

Six months after I was discharged from Rusk, I was able to go back to work at the accounting firm BDO Seidman. I started part time, three half days per week, as recommended by the vocational therapist.

Since I was still going for outpatient therapy, it took me one year to gradually work my way up to full time. After working there for two years, I left to work for a small CPA firm in Brooklyn, NY for another two years. I then moved to Long Island, and worked for a larger firm for almost five years.

When I left there, I started my own accounting practice. I am currently a Certified Public Accountant and have been self-employed for over fifteen years. I am so happy I was able to prove the doctors wrong. Not only am I able to "function as an accountant," I'm also able to run my own accounting practice.

The one physical issue I still deal with from the accident is the pain in my neck. I suffer from osteoarthritis, which causes stiffness and an inability to turn my head fully in either direction. It has gotten much better since the accident, when it was tilted to one side and did not move at all. I attribute the improvements to chiropractic treatments and Bikram Yoga.

Against the advice of my doctors and physical therapists, I started chiropractic treatment six months after being discharged from the hospital. The results have been truly amazing.

I first met with Dr. Musnik, located in Howard Beach, NY. His specialty is known as The Pierce-Stillwagon Technique which requires the use of a table with pelvic and cervical drop pads. It was a very gentle type of adjustment. After only a few months of treatment, at one time per week, my neck started to improve and have increased movement. Also, the problem I had in my shoulder, with my scapula winging out, has completely healed. This was the same problem that was diagnosed in the *torture test* that the doctor said couldn't be healed.

After a few years of that type of treatment, my neck was moving much better, but I still had severe muscle spasms in that area. I then met with Dr. Castro, located in Smithtown, N.Y. He is a chiropractor with a specialty in ART or Active Release Technique. He used this technique to break down muscle adhesions in my neck and back. This did wonders for me and my neck has continued to become more mobile.

After a few more years of being treated by him, I thought I had reached my peak. Although my ability to move and turn my head was still limited, it improved dramatically from where I started.

About two years ago, a friend referred me to Dr. Gucciardo, located in Howard Beach, N.Y. His specialty is in upper cervical treatments. Once again, my ability to move my neck continued to improve.

It must be more than mere coincidence that his office is located half a block from the scene of my accident. It's as if I was brought back there to heal.

I have been going for chiropractic treatment for over twenty-five years and I'm still improving.

The Bikram yoga has also been amazing. I started this about fourteen years after the accident. This ninety minute class is done in a room heated to about 105 degrees. After my very first class, I was able to move my head and neck better than I had since the accident. The heat and the stretching continue to give my neck more flexibility. I attend class two to three times a week. If I go less than that, my neck starts to stiffen up and becomes painful. I've practiced hot yoga at various studios throughout Long Island.

Since surviving this accident, I have become somewhat of a "health nut." I plan on doing everything in my power to stay healthy and avoid being under a doctor or nurses' care, or lack of it, again. No food or vice could be worth spending even one day in a hospital.

To further reinforce this thought, I met a CPA from Coopers and Lybrand, one of the big eight accounting firms of that time, during my stay at Rusk. He was an overweight gentleman who had had a heart attack. He knew I was a new CPA and he warned me, "Be careful not to get so busy with work that you don't take care of yourself. It's not worth it."

I read recently that when the Dalai Lama was asked what surprised him most about humanity, he answered, "Man. Because he sacrifices his health in order to make money. Then he sacrifices money to recuperate his health."

I'm determined to keep my health a priority in my life.

The most important thing I learned was to never give up. There were many times throughout my hospital stay that I felt sick, exhausted and beaten. However, after any minor or major setback, I only became more determined. I didn't want to let anything beat me. I think the definition of perseverance best describes me at that time: the quality that allows someone to continue trying to do something even though it is difficult.

I also realized how I grew so much strength from family and friends to help me get through that ordeal. I thank God that I was surrounded by people who loved and cared about me. I also thank God for giving me the strength and will power to keep pushing forward. There's not a day that goes by that I don't think about what I've been through. But I know for a fact that no matter what happens, I have a loving family, and loyal strong friends who I can always count on.

About two months after I was discharged from the hospital, I reconnected with a girl I knew when I was 16. We had lost touch for a few years. We started dating and quickly fell in love. She was very special and caring and gave me my first taste of unconditional love. We got married three years later in 1992. They were, by far, the best three years of my life.

A few months after we were married, my wife, GeneAnn, started getting some unexplained symptoms and eventually was diagnosed with Scleroderma. This is a chronic autoimmune rheumatic disease that primarily affects the skin. If I had never lived through my experience, I would not have been able to love and support her throughout her illness. I also learned how to challenge and stand up to the doctors, which I needed to do quite often. I never gave up, hoping she would get well. I believe my attitude also encouraged her not to give up.

Unfortunately, the disease was too strong for her, and she died in 2001, nine years after we were married. At the time, I thought I could never continue living without her nor did I want to. Once again, I received love and support from my friends and family and I again, decided not to give up and try to live my life to the fullest.

You can never choose what life events will or will not happen to you. But you can decide how you will react to those events. I decided to never give up

Yoga in Costa Rica - 2009

Yoga in New York - 2014

WE NEED YOUR HELP NOW!!

-PLEASE READ THIS LETTER-
"IT COULD SAVE YOUR LIFE"

West Hamilton Beach
VOL.
FIRE DEPT.
& AMBULANCE
BUSINESS 843·9863   EMERGENCY 843·1716

Fleeing Car Almost A Killer
Hamilton Volleys Rescue Driver

Dear Volunteers,

You guys are great. You saved my life. I was in a very serious car accident near Crossbay Blvd. I found out that you guys were there in a few minutes. If I would have had to wait for the 911 Ambulance I would not have made it. I want to come there and personally thank the crew who came to my aid. Also, I am not working yet, but when I do start I would like to make contributions to that life saving organization. You guys deserve so much and I am sure you get very little. Well, I give you all my praise and thanks for being there when I need YOU. As I said in the beginning of this letter, YOU GUYS ARE GREAT.

Thank you,
Joey Parenti

My thank you letter to the volunteers

Reactions

"When I heard what happened, it was of course impossible in those days to reach anyone. I jumped on a plane, slept at the hospital and a friend's house. I don't even remember if you were conscious when I left a few days later." **Steven B, Glenwood Springs, CO**

"It was after 12:45 a.m. I was sleeping on my couch when Joe D. called to tell me that you got hit really bad and that you were pronounced dead but they brought you back to life and you were at Jamaica Hospital and to get there now. I made it to the hospital and we met in the lobby. Everyone was crying; it was horrible! All I remember everyone saying is we have to get him to a better hospital. We stayed until the CT scan results came in but we couldn't see you. It was a sad, sad night. We all prayed like we never prayed before!" **Carla M, Franklin Square, NY**

"I was waiting tables in an Italian restaurant upstate when I got the news about Joey's accident. After my mother received a phone call from Joey's sister, she immediately called me at the restaurant to tell me Joey was in a bad car accident and was in the hospital. I remember my throat swelling up and not being able to ask about the details. A rush of thoughts and questions went through my head. Was he already dead and they just weren't telling me? Was he in pain? Was he going to be crippled? I pulled myself together and got back to work. I guess the thoughts of what Joey was going through preoccupied my mind. I was screwing up orders and customers were complaining. This waitress, Colleen, who I was good friends with, knew something was wrong. She pulled me aside and asked is everything ok? Trying not to cry, I just looked down at the floor and told her my best friend had been involved in a very serious car accident. For the rest of the night, she helped me out with my tables and got me through my shift. After the restaurant closed, I gave her a ride home, which gave us a chance to talk. Once we were in her driveway, I broke down and cried. I told her how Joey loved to dance and what if he never can after this. It helped having her there to let it all out. Colleen and I dated for several months after that. Joey and I joke about how he was ultimately responsible for this love connection. Over the past thirty years Joey and I have had some great times and I'm glad he's still around to laugh about this. After all he's been through, he's an inspiration and a true friend." **Michael H, Rockland County, NY**

"I was in my dorm room at Stonybrook University when my girlfriend called me and said 'JP died.' I was so confused, knowing JP was a young and healthy guy. So I asked her, 'What are you talking about? Are you sure?' She then told me he had been in an awful car accident and had died. I was really upset and trying to deal with all these emotions while going to classes and studying. I was so happy when I found out a few days later that you were still alive. It was a very odd experience, trying to come to terms with the fact that one of your friends died and then finding out he was still alive." **Jason K, Freehold, NJ**

"I was working that horrible night at Lenny's Clam Bar. We were going out after work and I was trying to get JP to join us. This was the most devastating scene I have ever witnessed, for we really thought we may have lost a good friend. I remember praying and crying out to Joe D. in the restaurant. We all stayed quiet and somber for the next month working at the restaurant not knowing if you were improving. All we could do was hope and pray for you, our great friend." **Tom C, St Louis, MO**

"I remember Anthony T. telling me that he heard the boom from his bedroom and ran out to see the accident a block away and he thought about how he had just chatted with you the day before. I remember being panicked and rushing to the hospital to get straight answers, to clarify rumors about brain dead or coma or paralyzed. At the hospital, I saw you with the tracheotomy and all the equipment, but somehow you didn't look uncomfortable, your face was always looking leftward towards the door as if to greet your friends and family. And though I was still worried, I had my faith that you would pull through. Most of the days I was there, I remembered talking with all of your family, but I found the most comfort and looked forward to speaking to Mike's wife Diane. I think she had the most faith and my outlook for you was best at those moments. Your CPA results came in and my hopes and prayers eventually came true that you would still be able to practice. There were times I cried and other times that I left and we talked about stories about you, kind of like a funeral." **Greg S, Amityville, NY**

"The morning after the accident, my friend called to let me know there was this horrible car accident on her corner and someone was killed. When she described the car I said, 'that sounds like Joe Parenti's car' and she said, 'Yes, I think that was his name.' I called the local rectory to find out if anyone died the night before. The priest let me know that you were alive and in Jamaica Hospital. We drove together to the hospital but only the priest was allowed in to say a prayer since you were in critical condition. I was sitting on the floor in the hallway with your mom when he came out of your room and told me 'He's in very bad condition.' I told him, 'If he was meant to die, he would have died last night. He's gonna pull through this.'" **June M, Howard Beach, NY**

"I received a phone call from my mother telling me something happened around the corner. She was explaining the details and then said I might know the person. She mentioned your name. I was in shock. I remember going to the hospital and wanting to see you right away, but we were told to wait a few days. When I finally got back to the hospital that week, I remember seeing your brother and the rest of your family. I couldn't even look at you, I didn't even recognize you. I remember meeting up with friends talking about you and how you were my first friend in school." **Michael S-Bethpage, NY**

"It was Tuesday morning, December 6, 1988, about 7:30 a.m. but I remember it as if was just yesterday. I was working in my office at a new company as a young engineer. My phone rang. It was my mother. Listening to my mom for just 10 seconds, my mouth dropped, my face went flush, and my eyes reddened and teared. I hung up the phone and started to leave my office. My associate, a few feet away said, 'Tony, what is it?' I couldn't talk. I mumbled something to him like 'gotta go...accident', and ran out of the office. My mom had told me 'Your good friend, Joey Parenti was in a terrible collision late last night on 91st Street. He had been revived several times and he is in a coma at Jamaica Hospital.' I don't remember the 20 mile drive to the hospital. With my emotions in high gear, and my brain in complete disarray, not processing, the drive probably took 5 minutes at 100 mph, rushing to see my best friend. I couldn't get there fast enough. I remember walking into the waiting area being met by Joey's family. I was in full tears, unable to speak, but all that came out was 'wha..., wha...' His brother, Mike, also my best friend, just hugged me. We sat and prayed. Over the following weeks, months and years, all his close friends and relatives were by Joey's side supporting his long, slow, very difficult, journey to recovery. From hospital to hospital, institute to institute, I was by Joey's side, just like the 10 years before as childhood pals. And today, we're still best friends...26 years later." **Anthony M, New Hyde Park, NY**

ACKNOWLEDGEMENTS

This book would not have been possible if not for The West Hamilton Beach Volunteer Fire Department. Without their quick response and expert care, I would not be alive today. To show my gratitude, a portion of the profits from the sale of this book will be donated to their organization. A special thanks to Billy, the paramedic, for bringing me back to life...more than once.

Thank you to my brother Michael for being my bodyguard in the hospital by standing up to and challenging the doctors. I would not be here if not for your love and concern. And a special thanks to Diane, his girlfriend at that time and now wife, for supporting him while he stayed with me every night for four months.

Thank you to my sister Diana and my mother Marie, for putting your lives on hold to care for me better than I could have ever dreamed of.

Thank you to my sister Lisa, for travelling to the hospitals in New York so often while you lived in Georgia and for convincing me to seek chiropractic care.

Thank you to my girlfriend Lily, for proofreading and re-reading my manuscript so many times and for encouraging me to write this book. I would not have finished it without your love and support. I'm so happy that we found each other again.

Thank you to my nephews Austin and Paul, for your all your input and support in telling my story.

Thank you to my friend Lorraine, for translating my scribble from a twenty-three year old notebook.

Thank you to my friend Charles Casillo, author of "The Marilyn Diaries," for your guidance and assistance in writing and finishing this book.

ABOUT THE AUTHOR

Joseph Parenti is a self-employed CPA and creator of the website Miracleon91st.com. Joseph is committed to living a healthy lifestyle and passionate about motivating others to do the same. Joseph enjoys working out, practicing Bikram yoga, dancing and living life to the fullest. He lives in Long Island, New York. You can follow him on his Facebook page, Miracle on 91st Street, or on his blog at Miracleon91st.com.